W9-AHS-685

LIGHT IN THE DARKNESS

895

LIGHT IN THE DARKNESS

Recollections and Reflections of an Orthodox Christian in Russia Today

by
SERGEI FUDEL

Translated by
SOPHIE KOULOMZIN

ST VLADIMIR'S SEMINARY PRESS
Crestwood, New York 10707
1989

Library of Congress Cataloging in Publication Data
Fudel, Sergei 1901–1977.
[Selections. English. 1989]
Light in the darkness: recollections and reflections of an Orthodox Christian in Russia today / Sergei Fudel; translated by Sophie Koulomzin.
    p.   cm.
Translated from Russian.
Includes glossary.
ISBN 0–88141–075–6 $6.95
1. Spiritual life—Orthodox Eastern authors. 2. Fudel, Sergei, 1901–1977. 3. Soviet Union—Church history—1917– . I. Title.
BX382.F83213   1989   89–6283
281.9'47—dc20   CIP

LIGHT IN THE DARKNESS
Translation © Copyright 1989

by

ST VLADIMIR'S SEMINARY PRESS
All rights reserved

ISBN 0–88141–075–6

Typeset at St Vladimir's Seminary on an IBM PC AT computer
and a QMS PS 810 laser printer using Ventura Publisher 2.0
in Times Roman 11pt on 12.5pt

PRINTED IN THE UNITED STATES OF AMERICA

TABLE OF CONTENTS

Introduction

Christians of the Western World are interested in the nature of religious life in Soviet Russia and are often bewildered by it. Tourists and visitors see the crowded churches, are impressed by the beautiful singing, the elaborate ritual, and the devotion of the people attending the services. The majority of the churchgoers are elderly, and very traditional in their piety. Most of them have been subjected to calculated government and cultural anti-religious propaganda all their lives. Atheism has been hammered into them in school, from kindergarten through college, at work through administrative measures, and in their homes in books, magazines and newspapers, and constantly on radio and TV, yet there they stand, plain simple people, crowding the churches to capacity at every service. Is their devotion part of real life today, or is it an archaic remnant of the past? And among the elderly more and more often we see a few young people, a few children and some cultured faces of the new "intelligentsia." What is the quality of spiritual life that has proved so indestructible, and so viable, bearing seeds after seventy years of suppression?

I believe that we can come to a better understanding of historical periods and of their meaning through that quality of individual life which we call "holiness." The holiness of great saints helps us to understand our historical past. The study of the lives of Saints Sergius of Radonezh, of Saint Francis of Assisi, of Saint Seraphim of Sarov helps us to better understand the inner meaning of the historical process that took place in their time. For saints are not simply good, kindly, moral people, but men and women whose personality reflects the vision and light of a life greater than the individual existence. We can better understand the meaning of the spiritual process going on in Russia today by learning to know the thoughts and reflections of men and women in whom there is something of real holiness. Religion lives in Russia today through the people who toil, suffer, overcome difficulties, think, love, rejoice, bear hardships, ask questions, try to find answers, and remain faithful to their vision of God.

The writings of Sergei Fudel (1901–1977) presented here for the first time in English, allow us to take a look at the thoughts and inner life of one such humble, little-known, saintly man who lived and died in the Russia of today.

Sergei Fudel was the son of a Moscow parish priest. He was never ordained to the priesthood and had no formal theological education. He remained in Russia all of his life. At the age of twenty he was arrested for the first time for his religious activities and, from then on, spent the greater portion of his life in prisons, labor camps, and exile, a total of some twenty-five years. He married and had two sons. He died peacefully in the small provincial town of Pokrov on March 7, 1977.

In his youth, Sergei Fudel's thinking and character were greatly influenced by his father, Joseph Fudel, an Orthodox priest. For many years Father Joseph Fudel had served as chaplain in a large pre-revolutionary Moscow prison, giving all his time and strength to serving the spiritual and material needs of a flock of over two thousand criminals. During the last years of his life he was appointed to a small Moscow parish. He was always strongly influenced by the "elders" of the Optino Monastery and was a frequent visitor there, taking his young son with him. Among Father Joseph's friends were the great theologians and thinkers of his day: C Leontiev, Father Paul Florensky, and Father Sergius Bulgakov (not yet a priest). He belonged to the enlightened Russian clergy of pre-revolutionary days who were painfully conscious of the spiritual stagnation of their time, the torrid atmosphere before a great storm. Father Joseph Fudel died in 1918.

Sergei kept a deep and loving memory of his father and, through him, was drawn into the orbit of the great Russian Christian thinkers of the day. During the long years of his imprisonment and exile he came in touch with many victims of religious persecution, including bishops, priests, monks and nuns. These contacts were his real theological education, the school in which his spirit was formed and in which he gained a deep understanding of life, of suffering, of evil, and of the Church.

While still in prison, Sergei Fudel began to write, with little hope of ever seeing anything published. He wrote about the spiritual heritage of Russia's past and its possible future, about Dostoyevsky, about the Optino Monastery and its elders, about his father. In the seventies several of his manuscripts reached the outside world. His biography of Father Paul Florensky was published in France by the YMCA Press, under the pseudonym of F Udelov. Some articles also appeared in France in the magazine *Vestnik*. His memoirs and reflections, entitled *At the Walls of the Church*, were published in one of the most remarkable "Samizdat" publications, the almanac *Nadezhda* (Hope). Nine issues of the almanac were prepared in Soviet Russia, eventually smuggled out, and printed abroad, before Zoia Krakhmal-nikov, its editor, was arrested in 1981. For easier readability I have allowed myself to group Fudel's writings under separate headings according to their subject matter. The present booklet is a translation of this text, with very slight abbreviations.

Very few facts are known about Sergei Fudel's personal life. People who met him told me he was a shy, retiring man, very unaggressive in expressing his opinions, perhaps sub-dued by the years of persecution. A man who knew him wrote, "His spirit was serene, peaceful. To stand next to him at the time of prayer, was a joyful experience, hard to forget and impossible to describe. Not only did he have a warm and loving heart, but he gave warmth to the hearts of many others" (A Burdeyev, *Vestnik*, #121).

Rather amazingly, Fudel was able to keep in touch with the life and thinking of the Western world. In his journal he quotes books and authors, both foreign and of the Russian diaspora, and he has no hesitation in recognizing which of them are meaningful and valid in the light of Christian experience in Soviet Russia. His judgment is intellectual and at the same time he has a simple, childlike faith in the manifestations of divine power in daily life, and in the miraculous. One of the most striking aspects of his thinking is his frank facing of the evil that exists even within the church enclosure. He knows what it means to betray the Church, to pervert Church teachings, to break commitments. He knows evil and is not frightened. He believes evil within the church enclosure is evil against the Church, not of the Church. His criticisms are frank and daring, but always understanding, always inspired by love. His thinking is permeated by his experience of Russian Orthodox liturgical life. This may make some passages difficult reading for the Western Christian, but it does show the importance of liturgical services in the preservation of Christian faith in Russia.

Sergei Fudel belongs to the generation of Russian Christians whose entire adult life was spent during the years after the Russian Revolution of 1917. Men and women like him were carriers of old Russian spiritual tradition who faced the challenge and trials of new times and kept their faith alive. Today there is a younger generation in Soviet Russia which experiences a reawakening of interest in religion. Because of people like Sergei Fudel — bearers of light that shines in the darkness — they are helped in their spiritual growth.

Sophie Koulomzin
Sea Cliff, New York
1988

1

The Church, What is it?

We experience a sense of "life incorruptible" when we find ourselves close to the real holiness of the Church. Such moments do not last long, and when we experience them we can never be sure whether we ourselves are actually within this holiness. For a short and joyous instant we can feel that we stand at the blessed walls of the Church. Our existence within the Church is not our right, it is always a miracle of unexpected joy.

✣ ✣ ✣

The Church is a mystery of overcoming lonely solitude. Overcoming solitude must be experienced realistically. Attending a church service, you come close to the wall of God's Church only when a ray of love slowly but inexorably melts the ice of your loneliness. Then you stop noticing that which seemed to build a barbed wire fence around you, the real or imaginary lack of faith of the priest, the viciousness of the old women on the watch for proper church behavior, the barbaric curiosity of two gaping youths who happened to drop in, the commercial arguments around the sale of candles. Then, through all of this you reach out to the blind soul of people, to the human being who in a minute may hear better and more clearly than you the voice of Jesus Christ, Man and God.

Quite often we come to realize very unexpectedly that the Church is an all-human reality. One day, riding on the subway, I saw a woman sitting with a little girl of about two in her lap. Over the mother's shoulder the child stretched her blue-mittened hand to the brake handle, almost, but not quite, reaching it. Suddenly I noticed a well-dressed young man watching her too. Our eyes met and we both smiled. We both sensed that the little mitten was a pure treasure of our common humanity. The brake handle was a symbol of some outside power, a key to the cold knowledge of good and evil, but the blue mitten stood for warmth, for the mysterious, unselfconscious innocence of childhood. We smiled to each other as if we were not strangers; for a moment, we were of one warm, innocent heart. This is what the Church is.

✠ ✠ ✠

"You are God's temple," says Apostle Paul. There is a special prayer in our prayerbook that speaks of our own self as a temple: "Let Thy power come down on me, Thy sinful and unworthy servant, and let it fortify my temple through the gospel of Thy holy teaching ... In Thine unfathomable graciousness preserve my body and soul, my mind and my thoughts, as a temple withstanding all enemy snares" (Prayer of the 12th Kathisma).

✠ ✠ ✠

Two little boys enter a church; one is about six, the other, younger. The little one has probably never been inside a church before and the older one is guiding him around. They stop at the image of Christ crucified. "What's that?" breathlessly asks the little one, his eyes wide open. The older answers confidently, "That's for truth!"

In the hymns to Saint Sergius of Radonezh we say that

"he lived his bodily life spiritually, spent his days on earth as if it were heaven, communed with people as if they were angels, and his own world was otherworldly." Perhaps we do not want to live like this, but each one of us must try, within the measure of his strength, to live on earth in this heavenly way.

✠ ✠ ✠

There is a difficult antinomy, a contradiction, between the belief in the spiritual progress of history which results in a moral transfiguration of humanity and a cold and self-satisfied withdrawal from the world. Both are contrary to the Gospels. On the one hand, faith in the progress of history is either a secularistic fraud, or a naive and silly idealism. Even the early Christian belief in a holy millennium, a period of Christ's reign on earth in human history, does not deal with all of humanity. According to the book of Revelation it will be a millennium of "the camp of the saints," a "beloved city," surrounded by enemies. Heliasm is a belief that, before the end of history, the Church will be granted a period of time when its holy life will be separated and kept safe from the evil still reigning in the world.

On the other hand, there is no worse distortion of Christianity than a cold and self-satisfied concentration on one's own salvation, renouncing all struggle and suffering for the pains of the world, an un-loving and thus un-Christian withdrawal from concern for the world.

This antinomy, this contradiction, is resolved through the cross of our Lord Jesus Christ "by which the world has been crucified to me, and I to the world" (Ga 6:14).

Our renouncing the world is pleasing to God only when, through it, we take into our heart the whole world, or, in other words, only when we renounce the world for the sake of saving it.

We have to realize the separateness of the world from the Church. We have no right to ignore the fact that the world does not believe in the Church and sets itself in opposition to it. The last talk of Jesus with His disciples, as recorded by John, is the Lord's testament to His Church. Jesus says that His Church will remain in the world, surrounded by unbelief and hatred: "... the Spirit of truth, whom the world cannot receive, ... you know him (Jn 14:17) ... yet a little while and the world will see me no more, but you will see me (Jn 14:19) ... if you were of the world, the world would love its own but because you are not of the world, but I chose you out of the world, therefore the world hates you (Jn 15:19) ... you will weep and lament, but the world will rejoice (Jn 16:20) ... in the world you will have tribulations, but be of good cheer, I have overcome the world" (Jn 16:33).

The Lord overcame the world through His suffering love for that very same world.

There is another passage in the Lord's testament: "Judas, not Iscariot, said to him, 'Lord, how is it that you will manifest yourself to us, and not to the world?' Jesus answered him, 'If a man loves me, he will keep my word, and my Father will love him, and we will come to him and make our home with him" (Jn 14:22–23). The disciple, brought up in a Messianic "happy ending" kind of faith, is confused because Jesus so clearly proclaims at this last supper that He will be the head of the Church, but not of the world. The Lord's answer dissolved all illusions about the Lord's "manifestation to the world." "A home" is created in the world and in and through this "home" Christ will be "manifested" to the world.

The whole world, constantly, every day and every instant, is being called to become part of the Church. The Church wants to become the whole world and it wants the whole world to become the Church. But we see that the world wants to remain on its own, by itself.

I could mention many dear people who have helped me, but perhaps it is best to keep silent, for fear that any word of mine may be said in a way that would trouble them. I will always remain grateful to all those who, in one way or another, consciously or unconsciously, were opening the doors of the Church for me during my entire life. Sometimes it was just a crack, sometimes it was a great deal.

This is the frightening character of our times. there are so few left of those "who open doors." It is said, "Save me, O Lord for holiness has grown poor."

✠ ✠ ✠

Khomyakov said, "each one of us is searching for that which the Church possesses always."

The holiness of the Church is not allegory because it lives in real people, and for real people, even if "there are only two or three gathered in My name."

Are we really part of these two or three? Are we looking for the grace of the Holy Spirit which makes us become part of the Church, which enlightens us, makes us holy? Do we even know that we should pray for the acquisition of the Holy Spirit, for the gifts of holiness?

✠ ✠ ✠

Holiness is the reality of our communion with the Holy Spirit. The reality of the Church lies in its holiness, in its being filled with the Holy Spirit in all its members. If the Church is not holy, then it is not one, not catholic, not apostolic.

We know that very often representatives of the Church are not holy. Because of this, people have less and less faith in the Church and the Church means less and less for the world. International religious conventions and appeals for social reforms and action do not attract people. There have been too many highly intellectual conferences, too many wise programs, during the bitter course of our history. Man knows that he can be saved by God only, through His suffering and His power, which we must make our own through love and effort (*podvig*). This is why the decrease of holiness in the world and in the Church is so great. The world rejects love and rejects effort.

When the circle draws to its close, there will remain on earth, unconquered, the "two or three" holy ones, the Church of Christ; and the light of their holiness will be too strong for human history. This will be the end of history. These unconquerable "two or three" will show that the Kingdom of Heaven and the Will of God are fulfilled in them "on earth as in heaven" and that all of humanity could have been such as they.

The Church truly lives. Its life is a mystery, first of all because of its invincibility. There is also another aspect of the Church, a kind of "external court of the temple." The Church of God lives but there is an enclosure around it. The true Church expresses itself outwards. It lives not only within itself, but also exists externally in human history. Yet there are also things that exist as "churchly" externally, but are "full of hypocrisy and iniquity within" (Mt 23:28).

> Then I was given a measuring rod like a staff, and I was told, "Rise and measure the temple of God and the altar and those who worship there, but do not measure the court outside the temple for it is given to the nations and they will trample over the holy city ..." (Rv 11:1-2)

Church history consists in the coexistence of these two aspects, beginning with the Last Supper itself. They also co-exist in church pre-history, the Old Testament. "Woe to you hypocrites and white washed tombs," says the Lord; yet in that same enclave of Old Testament pious ritual live John the Baptist, the men who became Apostles, and Mary, the Mother of Jesus, who is the very essence of the Church.

During the course of its history the "external court" of the Church may be reduced almost to nothing, but at other times it can grow larger and be filled with darkness.

In the early days of Christianity the Christians somehow remained within the Old Testament Temple, they observed its rules and prayed together with the same members of the Jewish faith who had crucified the Lord. Of course, from the very beginning, "they broke bread in their homes" (Ac 2:46), that is, they celebrated the sacrament of the Holy Eucharist separately.

This again gives us an example of the coexistence of light and darkness. Will not the end of Christianity be the same? Do we not witness today a constantly speeding-up process that shapes the "external court" of the Church?

✛ ✛ ✛

Father Paul Florensky used to say in the twenties that he admitted the possibility that a local, national church would cease to exist. The promise to remain invincible to the gates of hell was given to the Ecumenical Church, not to the church of a given country. Similar thoughts were expressed by Bishop Theophan the Recluse. In the 1870's, at a time of seeming prosperity for the Russian Church, he wrote "The younger generation is kept within limits by memories of their childhood, of their parents' traditions. But what will happen to their children? What will keep them in bounds? I believe that within a generation or two our Orthodox faith will disappear" (*Letters concerning Christian life*, 1886, pp. 70–71).

Father Seraphim Batiugov saw this decline quite clearly, but he believed at the same time that the Russian Church, not only the Ecumenical Church, will experience a spiritual rebirth. He greatly appreciated a little known work by L Tikhomirov, *The Teachings of the Book of Revelation on the Seven Churches*. In it the term "the church of Philadelphia" is interpreted to apply to the spiritual end of history which is now drawing near.

I remember his saying "It is truly an inspired book!" The term "church of Philadelphia" became for him a term symbolizing church renaissance. Another priest used this term when speaking of individuals whose spiritual character fitted the description given to the church of Philadelphia in the Book of Revelation. "You can believe this woman," he would say, "she is a true Philadelphian."

Perhaps all this is true. Perhaps unnoticeably for us, this new period of spiritual history is beginning, like waves in water which soundlessly overtake each other. Perhaps someone is already keeping "the word of patient endurance" and holding on to the treasure of grace within him, recognizing it in his very sinfulness. Perhaps, even now, out of the thousands of nominal Christians, there are being chosen those in whose hearts there is no impurity, no deceit, no fear — those three great sins of the modern church people. Those chosen ones will "follow the Lamb wherever He goes" (Rv 14:4).

✛ ✛ ✛

There is so much we do not know, but one thing is clear: the night of history is drawing to its end. Father Florensky said once: "We can see the glimmering light of dawn on the domes of the church."

Maybe the main task of our generation, of those who are leaving, is to transmit to the young Christians this awareness of the coming dawn, a sense of accomplished time. We grew up under the influence of Optino Monastery, of Dostoyevsky, of Solovyev, of Father Florensky. One of the best memories from the days of my adolescence are the Holy Week evening services in springtime Moscow, when they sing "Behold the Bridegroom cometh." On such days the epoch to which we belonged was taking farewell of something, was preparing itself for something terrible and bright.

Our generation was not strong, the scope of our knowledge was very limited. We only knew that a period of history was coming to an end. Even the word "knowledge" is not accurate. As Alexander Blok said:

It is a dream, so living and so instant,
That Joy will come when we don't expect it
And that it will remain fulfilled.

2

Icons and Church Services: Joys and Difficulties

It is difficult to pray without icons. An icon focuses our prayerful attention, as a magnifying glass focuses diffused sunlight into a spot of intense brightness. Church Fathers teach that icons proclaim the reality of Christ's humanity. Rejecting icons means renouncing the reality of the Incarnation, i.e., the human nature of Jesus, God and Man.

Yet in our world today, prayer is experienced in strange ways. I was spending the night in a new section of Moscow. Out of the incongruously huge window I could see the cold panorama of endless new, modern buildings. There were no icons in the room, but I wanted to pray and stepped to the window. It was better to face that threatening Martian landscape, I thought, than to huddle in a corner pretending that nothing had changed. Suddenly, I felt that I was praying, easily and simply, as if really nothing had happened. I was praying as if the sky were my icon and it was so close. Suddenly, I felt that heaven is my home and the spaces around me are not frightening. I felt that man is free in his Christian faith.

✤ ✤ ✤

Christianity does not disappear when, speaking in terms of history, icons disappear. The doctrine of icons has an eternal meaning because it reflects the eternal truth of the Incarnation of God. But you may find yourself in a situation where there are no icons. I remember how we used to pray in prison, standing before a blank wall. It is both difficult and easy to pray in prison. Difficult because everyone stares at you and you cannot help being conscious of what they think: "bigot," "fraud." It is easy because, once you have overcome this sense of being watched, you really feel as if you were standing for a few minutes at "the gates of the Kingdom." In prison the Lord is at the very gates.

This is alien to the traditional Orthodox concept of prayer. It was made clear to me one day in prison. One of the inmates was a former "white" officer, a traditional old Russian. After watching me pray facing a blank wall, he asked me, "Are you a member of a sect?" I understood then that it is possible to pray without icons if there are none, but you cannot pray without humility. For if you do not have humility, then you judge a person who makes this kind of remark.

I remember a day in the early thirties, when they were closing down our parish church on Arbat Street. We learned of this two days ahead of the date set, and I came to say good-bye. No more services were held; the church stood empty. I went around venerating the icons, kissing them as if they were alive. Recently, looking at the icon of Christ, I remembered that day and again felt that the image of Christ is leaving the world in which we live. This is true both in the literal sense of the word and in the "iconographic" one. This is unbearably sad ...

People attending church services do not understand the

prayers and readings in old Slavonic very well. Sometimes the melodies of church singing make the text meaningful. Church singing is part of the Scriptures, it is a carrier of grace, a part of our Christian spirituality through the ages, and it can become a kind of key to difficult texts.

Quite an opposite effect is achieved by operatic and concert-like style of hymnography. The words of even familiar prayers become confused if the musical interpretation does not correspond to their Christian meaning.

One day, during the first week of Great Lent, as I was leaving the church before the end of the service, a woman stopped me, "Wait a minute ... They are going to sing the concert." A concert rendition of "Open to me the gates of repentance, O Giver of life!" Sounds rather like a "ballet rendition."

Operatic singing during church worship replaces the fellowship of prayer (*sobornost*) by a kind of entertainment. It deprives the faithful of spiritual guidance, the last kind of guidance we may have, for most of us are "sheep without a shepherd." Traditional church singing, its whole worshipful, meaningful musical order, guides the faithful in the experience of prayer. However, if the only thing that reaches the faithful are "musical effects" and vocalizations, then they are truly left to themselves instead of taking part in the mystery of worship.

In a recent article on the subject of "operatic singing" in church, published in the Journal of the Moscow Patriarchate, it was said, "The living concept of liturgical fellowship (*sobornost*) is gradually disappearing." Is this not the same as to say that the concept of "Church" is gradually disappearing from the life of the church?

✤ ✤ ✤

A priest, a sincere admirer of the liturgical rubrics of the Orthodox Church, spoke to me once with a real sense of frustration: "You cannot imagine how painfully conscious I am of the discrepancy between our funeral service and the actual circumstances of our life!"

The words of the very central hymn of the funeral service, "With the saints give rest to Thy servant ..." presupposes some sort of Christian faith on the part of the deceased, or at least a sparkle of repentance. Yet so often a priest is asked to celebrate the funeral service for someone who was a militant and active atheist, because the family of the deceased asks for it. How often funeral services are celebrated "in absentia," and the priest does not know the person he is burying, has never seen him; yet in the prayers he solemnly reads he calls him "my spiritual child." More and more often bishops authorize the church burial of those who have committed suicide.

Our liturgical rubrics have become fossilized at the level of the eleventh and twelfth centuries. What was true spiritual fatherhood then has now become a blasphemous conservatism.

✜ ✜ ✜

I have met priests who truly pride themselves because they know and strictly follow the liturgical rubrics of the church and yet are unbelievers. They follow a pattern established in medieval Byzantium, without being inspired by the faith of the Gospels. Without such faith "rubricism" becomes a spiritually unbearable dead weight. It covers up the threatening void of Church reality with a veil of Byzantine pompousness. "Everything is fine! We have sung all ten verses, not nine, and we used the proper tones!"

Archbishop Illarion, exiled to the Solovetsk labor camp,

speaking to a zealous priest, said with a kindly smile, "You, too, belong to the sect of 'rubricists'?"

Liturgical rubrics call us to a labor of prayer, i.e. to an effort of soul and body, not to pampering our bodily urges. In this sense it arms us for a spiritual battle. The schism of the twenties (*zhivotserkovtsy*) rejected liturgical rubrics because the concept of spiritual battle, of effort, was foreign to them.

Rubrics become dangerous when we forget that these are conditioned historically, when we dogmatize them, when we begin to "strain out a gnat and swallow a camel," when we replace Christian faith by Old Testament ritual.

We cannot neglect rubrics, but we must always remember that the Sabbath was made for man, not man for the Sabbath, and so too the rubrics. We can make changes in rubrics for the sake of love for people. Father Alexei Mechev used to say, "Love is greater than rubrics."

I know that the concept of the wisdom of love is very vague for those who do not love, but the Apostle James foresaw this when he wrote, "If any of you lacks wisdom, let him ask God who gives to all men generously and without reproaching and it will be given to him" (Jm 1:5).

Freedom of love and rubrics can be brought together only when everything in one's own life stands at the right place: the absolute first, the relative second. We are clearly told what is absolute, "Seek first His kingdom and His righteousness and all these things shall be yours as well" (Mt 6:33). The Kingdom of God is "within us," in the grace of the Holy Spirit. We must grieve most not for people's ignorance of church rubrics, but that so few of them know that acquiring the Holy Spirit of God must be the constant, daily, purpose of each Christian life. This is especially true today when our whole life drifts away from the fundamental truths and spiritual values of Christianity. This apostolic message was re-emphasized recently for us by Saint Seraphim of Sarov.

Freedom and rubrics can be fused into one only in true spirituality through the acquisition of the Holy Spirit. Only then can we reconcile belief that "rubrics are a holy church tradition" and the word of the apostle, "If you are led by the Spirit, you are not under the law" (Ga 5:18), including church rubrics in the "law."

Rationalistic disapproval of the formal worship prescribed by church rubrics is characteristic of some forms of Protestantism. It is a lack of faith in the Church, a lack of faith that its life can fill all kinds of forms, giving them eternal meaning.

In the fourth century, in the days of Basil the Great, the eucharistic bread was distributed to the faithful and they could take it home and keep it there for the use of the sick. It would be madness suddenly to re-introduce this early Christian custom today, when the spiritual level of the faithful is quite different and there is no real need for such a practice. But when circumstances change, when external events and spiritual needs demand it, the Church, in its simplicity and fullness of grace, replaces one form by another.

I remember how, in the fall of 1922, the bishops imprisoned in a Moscow prison, discussed the possibility of giving particles of eucharistic gifts to laymen condemned to exile in distant and isolated places. Later, while we were being transported north in a prison-train, a woman, at the request of her parish priest, brought into our boxcar the Holy Gifts intended for Bishop Thaddeus who was in our group.

✛ ✛ ✛

Of course, our ritual carries the heritage of Byzantium, and the sooner our church gets rid of it the better. I remember how I attended a service in a Moscow church, for the first time after several years of isolation. There was the bishop in his majestic vestments, the altar boys carrying the train of his rustling mantle, and the only association it brought to my mind was a courtly procession of Catherine the Great, a description of which I had read somewhere. What worries me is that our younger bishops seem to accept this pomposity, not only willingly, but with evident pleasure. Yet in pre-revolutionary times, I remember a well-known bishop's letter to the editor of a magazine, "I was horrified to read in your paper that they are planning to celebrate my 25th anniversary. We bishops are being solemnly celebrated every Sunday. We are solemnly met, supported as we move around, we are censed, accompanied, greeted in Slavonic, in Russian, in Greek. We really have enough of it."

We must realize that we are entering a new, non-Byzantine epoch of church life, that we must return to simplicity in our ritual, a simplicity in Christ.

✛ ✛ ✛

Recently, shortly after Easter, I attended a memorial service during which long lists of individual names were read. Usually it is a monotonous and tiring process, but this time, while the names were read, the choir kept singing Easter hymns, very quietly, over and over again. Such a practice is not prescribed by the church rubrics, yet it was truly a revelation, the names of the deceased became names of the living.

Is this not an example of how a living and holy church

tradition can be created quite unexpectedly and the Church can be illumined thereby?

The Church is apostolic not because it uses only those prayers, those words, those rules, that were established by the Apostles, but because, in addition to what it has received from the Apostles, it continues to receive throughout its history, through its saints, the same "Apostolic enlightenment" that was given to the Apostles and was transmitted by them.

The Apostles helped the Church grow, but on its historic road it is led by the One Who made the Apostles grow and Who said, "I am with you always, to the close of the ages."

Holy tradition is precisely this divine enlightenment which has been given to the Church and is being given again and again, now and ever and unto ages of ages. Yet, in addition to Tradition with a capital "T," there are many minor traditions, which include all kinds of local customs. Sometimes they are good ones, sometimes less than good and occasionally actually bad.

How simple was the apostolic liturgical service. In a disciple's house in Troas the disciples gathered together to break bread and Paul conversed with them a long while, until daybreak, and so departed for he was hastening to be in Jerusalem, if possible, on the day of Pentecost. He knew that suffering and imprisonment were awaiting him there (Ac 20:7, 11, 16).

Very different from this simple liturgy of the early Church is that celebrated by Saint Seraphim of Sarov, Saint Tikhon of Zadonsk, or Father John of Kronstadt, in the 18th and 19th centuries. The altar table is covered with gold and silver cloth, decorated with precious stones. The centuries-old ritual is complex, prayers are chanted that were unknown in apostolic times. Yet we see, though we dare not raise our eyes, that all these ornaments, all this ritual, are illumined by the same apostolic light of grace, as if their substance has become holy, as if we were still living in the early days of Christianity. When we stand in the presence of saints, of whatever century, we always tread the ground of the early Church. "The spirit bloweth where it listeth."

The Church not only remains in its essence the same as it lived in Troas, but it also moves towards Troas in its historical growth. It is important for us to realize, on one hand, the "sameness" of Troas and Sarov, and on the other that Troas is the beginning and the end of church growth, of church history.

✜ ✜ ✜

I often feel like warning young Christians who, in their enthusiasm, attach so much importance to external forms of piety, to special services, litanies, etc. "Seek first the Kingdom of Heaven," I want to tell them, "and all the rest will be given you, including all the special services." It is quite possible to discover and find delight in the long litanies and feel one has attained one's goal, yet what we are taught to seek is communion with God and communion with people.

Saint Ephrem of Syria says, "Monasticism is not the habit, not even the fact of being tonsured, it is a yearning for divine and heavenly living."

Such living is beyond our dreams, but we must all experience a yearning for the divine, a longing for the divine beauty of the Holy Spirit. Only this is the true purpose of Christian life about which Saint Seraphim of Sarov talks to Motovilov. Saint Seraphim proclaims this truth, calls us to it, sweeps away all deceptions of external piety and cold self-absorption. He affirms our constant and only purpose, uniting ourselves to God in our communion with Him.

In connection with the apparition of Christ to the human heart through art, I keep remembering Florensky's words about philosophical arguments to prove the existence of God. He said the best argument is Rublev's icon of the Holy Trinity. If this icon exists, then there is God.

People who believe in God in their own way, yet do not believe in the Church, often say, "Does God really need all this ritual? Why do we have to have all these formalities? We only need love, beauty and humaneness." A man, on his way to the woman he loves, seeing flowers, buys them or picks them and brings them to her, never stopping to think whether this is a formality or not. Yet this is the very concept of church ritual.

Love for God gives birth to the beauty and humanity of the ritual, which we lay, like flowers, at the feet of God. Faith is love, and the essence of Christianity is to be in love with God and to feel that the Church is His body which has remained with us and lives with us on earth. This feeling expresses itself in actions which we call ritual.

However, if only external and dead action remains, then such action will be sterile and self-deceptive, not only in Christianity, but in any sphere of human life, even in science. This truth should be clear to everyone.

Formalism and sanctimoniousness is not Christianity. Each one of us has to move along this long and narrow way from non-Christianity to Christianity, from artificial flowers to live ones.

Church sermons should be somehow at the level of the liturgical services. What the priest says, and how he says it, must not drag the faithful down from the level at which they had been placed by the service of worship.

Liturgical services are inspired, but we are afraid of the very word "inspiration," because poets loved it and we cannot find it in the *Typikon*. But listen to this, "... inspired by the Spirit he (Simeon) came to the Temple" (Lk 2:27). I am sure that if we were to attend a liturgical service in Apostolic days, when "inspired" people spoke in tongues, that is in foreign languages, and prophesied, we would say that it was a sectarian meeting.

✠ ✠ ✠

On a great holiday, in a large church in Moscow, I saw the priest come out with the chalice and say "With the fear of God and faith approach ..." Then he hurried down the steps of the ambo, carefully making his way through the huge crowd, into the side chapel, and there gave communion to the faithful. The hymn "Receive the body of Christ" was not sung. The reason was "One should not distract people's attention from the sermon." The sermon was preached by another priest, a learned theologian, in the main part of the church. Most of the parishioners were listening, and at the chalice, with the Holy Gifts of Christ, only a small group was standing in silence.

In another parish church I saw a similar situation. It was a feast day, too, and there were many communicants. Again, the priest came out, said, "Approach ..." and then turned back into the sanctuary. The choir sang "Alleluia!," as it is supposed to do after the faithful have received Holy Communion, and the deacon read the litany of thanksgiving for the Gifts, of which the faithful had not partaken. The liturgy ended, an additional special solemn service was chanted and only then — when all the solemnity was over, while the altar server was loudly scolding someone, and one could hear the jingling of coins being counted at the candle table, and a loud voice said "Business was good today, Ivan Petrovich!" — only then was the chalice brought out again and Communion given to those waiting for it. The reason: "We cannot detain the choir with too many people coming to Communion."

A deacon who served in another parish told me that he would sometimes be given a written message during the Saturday night service: "Don't drag out the petitions. There is a good movie tonight."

✛ ✛ ✛

An ancient icon is the best way to see heaven, to become conscious of heaven. Paintings by artists like Raphael or Vasnetzov do not let us reach out to heavenly reality. In terms of actual religious experience, their art is like the "false windows" that architects install in buildings for reasons of symmetry, but which let no light through. An icon is an attempt to penetrate into the mystery of divine beauty, while discarding all "prettiness." This mystery is beyond our natural perception. The icon speaks to us "not in plausible words of wisdom, but in a demonstration of the Spirit and power" (1 Co 2:4).

Of course we can pray looking at modern icons, but there is a time in our spiritual life when we are drawn to learn more about another world, when we want to look through the narrow, stylized art of an ancient icon into heavenly reality.

✛ ✛ ✛

I thought of "ritualistic conditioning" when I read the comment made on confession by Saint Ephrem the Syrian.

"If it is merely habit that sends you to the Physician, you will not receive healing. The all-merciful One wants love from the one who comes to Him, and if the supplicant brings love and tears he receives freely the gift of forgiveness."

Purity and holiness are attained through repentance. "Repentance is already a particle of holiness" says Father Alexander Elchaninov. At the end of the sacrament of penitence the priest says, "Accept and reunite this penitent to Thy Holy Church." This prayer for reunion is read every time, even if we come to confession daily. We commit sins every day and thus every day we need to be cleansed and reunited to the Church through repentance.

Inasmuch as we are unrepentant, we remain outside the Church. Yet our priests are "officially" obligated to go to confession once a year to an appointed regional confessor and many of them do this quite formally, merely to fulfill the letter of the rubrics. Thus, the very persons who have the greatest need for purification and holiness place themselves outside the path leading to it. It is as if they had received a patent for priesthood that takes care of everything.

Of course, there are exceptions, and God knows I have seen many of them. In the fifties there was a constant flow of priests coming to visit the spiritual advisors and elders of the Glinsky Hermitage. Today, many go to the monastery of the Holy Trinity in Zagorsk, to the Pechory Monastery in Estonia. I remember how Father Nicholas Golubtsov, after the death of his father confessor, diligently searched for another one.

3

The "Dark Double" of the Church

The sickness suffered by the Church is in all of us. If we realize sincerely that we belong to the sick part of the church community, we need not be afraid to admit the actual fact of sickness, as the Fathers of the Church were not afraid to do. Somehow, only then are we capable to feel, in the joy of our heart, the invincible holiness of the Church.

Metropolitan Anthony Bloom says, "The Church has a glorious aspect and a tragic one. Each one of us bears the aspect of the Church's infirmity. We are within the Church and yet we are on the way to it."

✜ ✜ ✜

A church service was ending in a suburban Moscow church. Everything seemed quite normal, the priest gave the final blessing. Then he stepped out of the sanctuary and began taking off his vestments. Suddenly there was dead silence and only his voice was heard, "For twenty years I have deceived you. Now I take off this attire!" People moved, some shouted, some cried. Everyone was upset, indignant. "Why then did he serve, even today?"

It is difficult to say how it would have ended, but suddenly a very young man stepped forward and said, "Why are we all so excited? Wasn't it always like this? Don't you remember Judas at the Last Supper?" Somehow these words reminded people that in the long history of the Church there had always existed its dark shadow, its "double," and somehow this helped us to understand and accept what took place. Judas had taken part in the Last Supper and this did not destroy the holiness of the Sacrament.

Yes, this is a kind of explication, but it does not take away the sorrow and the fear.

This took place in the twenties.

✛ ✛ ✛

A Moscow priest told me once, "I am celebrating the Divine Liturgy. In the sanctuary, to the right of me, stand two priests who are not serving today. On the left, our deacon and a member of the "parish twenty." To the right, an anecdote is being told. To the left, an argument goes on about building repairs. The choir sings "We praise Thee, we bless Thee ..." Finally I cannot stand it: "Fathers, I beg you ... Just stop talking for a minute ... I cannot ..."

Endless stories could be told of sins committed, of unbeliefs, of indifferences or formalism among the clergy. And it all takes place not in the long ago, but at the very time when Russian church leaders speak with assurance of its spiritual well-being.

Along with the immortal life of Christ's Church, evil has always existed, within the very enclosure of the Church. We must see this with our eyes open, always remembering that "the hand in the dish with Me, will betray Me." Saint Chrysostom was not afraid to recognize the spiritual sickness within his local church and to speak of it. Father John of Kronstadt said: "Unless you learn to recognize the spirit that kills, you will not learn to know the lifegiving Spirit. Only through the contrast of good and evil, of life and death, do we learn to understand both." And just now our Church lives through a time when it is especially important for Christians to clearly understand both life and death.

Father Valentine Sventitsky was in many ways a typical Russian, married priest, but he was also a real teacher of constant prayer. As early as 1925, right in the middle of Moscow, his sermons were a call to constant spiritual effort. He defended faith, but his greatest message was this constant call to prayer, to the burning life of the spirit. "Prayer builds walls around our monastery in the world," he used to say.

Summing up the problem of sin within the Church he said: "A sin within the Church is not a sin of the Church, but against the Church." Breaking away from the Church because of the moral derelictions we see in it is religiously foolish and reflects our inability to think things through. Anything wrong, distorted and impure that we see within the gates of the Church is not the Church. To avoid associating with it we do not have to leave the Church enclosure, we must simply refuse to participate in that which is evil. Then will be fulfilled the words "to the pure all things are pure" (Ti 1:15).

Church splits, schisms, are not merely foolish, they are caused by pride. One of the very first schisms, that of Montanism in the second century, affirmed that the Holy Spirit was not fully revealed in the Church and that they, the Montanists, were awaiting its complete revelation. The teaching was not caused by mere concern for better discipline, or an effort to attain greater purity in such matters as fasting, marriage, and readmission of fallen members. In truth, they denied the spirituality of the Church, believing themselves to be the only bearers of true spiritual life. Such is the mentality of the Old Believers in our times. What moral criteria can we apply to separate ourselves from the

Church? How can we draw formal and rational conclusions from a mystical reality? What earmarks can we apply to distinguish the "holy ones" from the "unholy ones" who have to be expelled? Who can see our inner sins and defects, our pride, viciousness, hypocrisy, coldness of heart and lack of faith? What is the criterion of "holiness" that would enable us to carry out a kind of moral chemical analysis?

Only the Holy Church is truly the Church, and its very being is a mystery which we cannot fully comprehend. Our eyes cannot see the Body of Christ. We may affirm that we can be members of the Church only "in truth," only "in the holiness of God," but we cannot assert which one of us, at any given moment, is or is not within this truth and holiness. This must be the reason why the Lord said in His parable: "Do not gather the weeds, lest you root up the wheat" (Mt 13:29). Either you or I, or he, or she, may be weeds at this moment, and in an hour any one of us may become wheat. Saint Irenaeus of Lyons said: "Every man is himself the reason why he sometimes becomes wheat and sometimes straw" (*Against Heresies*, Book 4, ch 4).

✠ ✠ ✠

A girl enters the church while a service of worship is going on. Her head is uncovered. She has no understanding of what she sees and she may be facing the wrong way. Right away, like hawks, zealous church-women assault her, zero-in on her, chase her out. Perhaps she will never enter a church again. A priest told me once that his daughter's atheism crystallized under the impression made on her by mean old women in church.

Nothing seems to be done about this, though I heard recently that a priest refused Communion to one zealot of rules and hater of people. "You think you are the mistress here?" he said sternly, addressing her in front of all the people in church, "You are not, the Mother of our Lord is mistress here!" Another Moscow priest called such women "Orthodox witches."

✛ ✛ ✛

The young ones who have just come into the Church, accept everything trustfully and uncritically. Then they may suddenly be hurt by that which I call the dark "double" of the Church, and they react desperately, may even return to godlessness. Yet, we have been told, "be wise as serpents and innocent as doves."

I knew a boy who during the "high tide" of his Christian faith would get up to pray secretly in the night, placing his one small icon on the edge of a pot with houseplants, just for a few minutes, because his father, a prominent atheist, might find it and throw it away. The young man had dreams of a monastic vocation, and nobody warned him, nobody prepared him. "Everything is just wonderful!" he was led to think. Then, suddenly, he was faced by the bitter heat of conflicts within the life of the Church. He could not hold out and left the Church.

We have to speak of the evil "double" of the Church from the very beginning, just as simply and clearly as the Gospel does. You must know of its existence and, in the Church, you must seek Christ, only Him because the Church is only Christ in His humanity, it is His Body. Then you will be given the wisdom of the heart to discern good from evil within the Church enclosure, you will be able to see the light that shines in the darkness and which the darkness cannot overcome.

✛ ✛ ✛

I knew a young priest who somehow managed in our time and place to visit the sick in the hospitals and bring them

Holy Communion. Anyone can understand how much
courage and faith this demanded. He could do it only because
he wore civilian clothes, was beardless and his hair was cut
short. He was truly a soldier out on the front line.

There is also another kind of priest. I remember waiting
one day in an archbishop's office. All kinds of people were
coming in and out, many of them priests. Suddenly, a well-
dressed, handsome man came in. He wore a smart raincoat,
an elegant hat, and a well-made suit. There was something
special about his appearance, his way of holding himself,
arrogant, self-assured, slightly contemptuous. He was carrying a briefcase. "Must be a reporter, or perhaps a well-
known artist, or sportsman!" I thought. Suddenly, he took
off his raincoat, opened the briefcase, took out a cassock, a
pectoral cross and unhurriedly put them on. I almost expected him to pull out a Byzantine beard and fix it on his
face.

Yes, there are really all kinds of priests. It is not the beard
that matters, it is the look in the eyes, the way a man holds
himself.

✥ ✥ ✥

A five-year-old boy was baptized in a parish church. A
week later he and his grandmother were walking when they
met the priest in the street. "Say 'hello' to Father," said
Granny, "he baptized you." "No," answered the boy, "he did
not baptize me, an angel baptized me and Father was lying
on a bench, with his hands tied down."

Of course, speaking of the "dark double" of the Church,
we can never make final judgments. Until the moment of the
Crucifixion no one knew the fate of the thief who acknow-
ledged Christ.

Father Vladimir Krivolutsky told me how he was once

asked to give Holy Communion to a dying man who had given up his priesthood many years ago. "When I had prepared everything for the sacrament on a small table next to his bed, he suddenly raised his head, drew a deep breath and said, "O Lord, O Lord! of what have I deprived myself?"

✠ ✠ ✠

We must learn to see everything, faith and unbelief, the Church and its dark "double." The Lord will give us wisdom to act rightly if our heart remains humble.

A wise French writer said, "It's more dangerous to lose belief in man's fall, than to lose faith in God." When man forgets his original sin he loses the sense of reality, human reality and church reality. He begins to believe idealistically and optimistically in a kind of general prosperity and closes his mind to the tragedy of the world and the suffering of the Church.

✠ ✠ ✠

I remember so well Sergei Mansurov (who later became a priest) reading his manuscript on church history to us. It was truly a story of the Church as a divine-human body, a story of the holiness and thinking of those who make up its very fabric. It was not a record of arguments and disagreements, of crimes committed by popes and patriarchs, of laymen's delusions. Yes, we must write about evils within the church enclosure, but we must treat them as a kind of anti-church matter, not as the Church itself. Unfortunately this is not being done, and it is so easy to completely lose one's way when studying church history.

Not only was Mansurov's church history impressive, but he himself was truly a saintly hero of our days. In the room where we were gathered to hear him speak hung portraits of

three great Russian laymen of the 19th century, Dostoyevsky, Khomyakov, Solovyev.

✤ ✤ ✤

"Strive for peace with all men and for the holiness
without which no one will see the Lord" (Heb 12:14).

"God's temple is holy and that temple you are" (1 Co
3:17) and "He who commits sin is of the devil" (Jude 3:8).
This means that the one who sins is not of the Church, not
of the temple, until he repents. For constant membership in
the Church we need constant repentance. This sheds light on
our need for constant, repentant prayer, "Father, I have
sinned against heaven and before you; I am no longer worthy
to be called your son, treat me as one of your hired servants"
(Lk 15:18-26).

4

Living in Faith

The fear of God comes from faith, not the other way round as some fearful people say. In the words of the psalm, "Let my heart rejoice in the fear of Thy name." You can rejoice only when you are glad, when you love. The fear of God is the beginning of wisdom but not of faith, because love is the beginning of faith. Outside of the loving faith we are left with the faith possessed by demons, "for the demons believe and shudder," that is they fear God. We, however, "believe because we love God" (Father Alexander Elchaninov).

We speak of the "fear of God" only as part of a loving faith, or, as the Apostle says, "faith active in works." Saint Basil says, "Nail our flesh to the fear of Thee and wound our hearts with the love for Thee" (Prayer of Basil the Great, Great Compline). Saint Tikhon of Zadonsk says, "Where there is no love, there is no faith," and thus there is no true fear of God, born from faith, without love.

✛ ✛ ✛

There are different kinds of fear. Saint Diodochus says that we should always include in our act of penitence and confession our involuntary sins, committed in knowledge or in ignorance. These sins are the cause of those vague fears we experience at the time of death, when our soul is separated from our body. "Yet we, who love the Lord, should seek to be free of all fear at the time of our end. Evil spirits consider the fearfulness of a human soul to be a sign of its participation in evil, as it is with them" (*Philokalia*, vol 3).

Our life is given its true meaning and its true vigor when we accumulate in our heart God's wealth, spiritual happiness. This happiness is joy in God, joy in our life in this God-created world, joy in fellowship with His people. This wealth is not our own, it belongs to God. This is a special joy because it is not ours, and we are thus delivered from ourselves. Such wealth is the treasure of the humble and most of us can only wistfully long for it.

Father Sergius Sidorov, whom I knew in the twenties when he was still only "Serezha," taught me the meaning of this kind of longing, not in so many words, but in the way he was. I learned from him that there are two truths that stand out like bright lights at the door leading to Christian life and to real happiness: a warm earthiness, a love for the earth which may sometimes even be romantic, and at the same time an equally warm feeling of being separated from the world, of standing aside.

Saint Ambrose of Milan says in his prayer, "Take away my heart of stone and give me a heart of flesh." Saint Isaac of Syria also prays, "O Lord, fill my heart with life eternal!" He said elsewhere, "Eternal life is comfort in God."

Living in faith means to strive to live in a constant awareness of life eternal. If we are not enlightened by such an awareness, we do not really live in faith, even though it may already be there in a kind of twilight state of "stony insensibility." Speaking of the myrrhbearing women, Bishop Ignatius Brianchaninov quotes their words, "Who will roll away the stone from the grave?" He says that "insensibility" is the stone which keeps intact all the other spiritual diseases until it is rolled away.

✢ ✢ ✢

Spiritual sensitivity is a sign that we are spiritually alive. Without spiritual sensitivity we remain in the realm of external formalities. A priest I knew, Father Alexei Zosimovsky, said, "We must keep our spirit burning always and everywhere," but he also said "we must never undertake spiritual heroic efforts for the sake of the spiritual gratification they give us. Their one purpose is to acquire true repentance."

"Always and everywhere" we must strive to acquire a sense of contrition and incipient love. We must search for Christ, and not for our own self, nor for some kind of state of spiritual bliss. To give us comfort is in the hands of God; of course, our heart yearns for such comfort.

✢ ✢ ✢

"When the cares of my heart are many, Thy consolations cheer my soul" (Psalm 94:19).

If there are no cares, no effort of repentance, there can be no "consolation," for what need is there then to be consoled?

If there is no effort, there is no Christian faith.

We must not be insistent in seeking consolation (though we can humbly yearn for it), but we should be insistent in our efforts to be truly Christian, to repent and to love. Then, unfailingly, you receive consolation which you feel with your whole heart.

Bishop Ignatius Brianchaninov prayed thus for a friend, "O Lord, let Leonid experience spiritual consolation so that his faith might become living, heartfelt, not merely an acceptance of words."

Archimandrite Guri wrote, "The Church is a felt experience of communion with God."

✠ ✠ ✠

The concept of living in the Church is difficult to explain, but easy to experience. "For those who understand all is reasonable; and for those who attain reason all is simple." It is merely living in the experience of the heart and not in the acceptance of words, not in philosophical reasoning, not in ritualistic conditioning. "The Church is not walls and a roof," said Saint John Chrysostom, "it is faith and life." We can also say that living in the Church means before all else tears of sorrow, because you cannot stand at the foot of the Lord's cross without tears.

✠ ✠ ✠

Pasternak has a poem about a man picked up in a city street by an ambulance and left in a hospital. He learns that he is dying. These are his thoughts:

And the sick man's thoughts welled up: 'O God,
How perfect your words are, how right!
All these people, these beds and these walls,
This death-night, the town in the night!
But I've taken a sleeping-draught now,
I'm crying, quite lost what to do:
Yet you know how these tears of emotion
Prevent me from looking at you.
And how wonderful here in the half-light
That's falling just over my bed
Just to know that my life and my fate
Are gifts without price you have shed!'
(*The Interlude* translated by Henry Kamen,
London, Oxford Press, 1962)

To me this sounds like the last words of Saint John Chrysostom, "Glory to God for all things!"

✠ ✠ ✠

Father Alexander Elchaninov writes, "Our young people today make a great mistake in thinking that Christianity is a system of philosophy which one can prove logically and which they, such as they are at the moment, can assimilate. No, Christianity is life."

So often we see a youngster embrace the Christian faith and accept it with fervor and delight. The new Christian thinks, "What a wealth of thought, after the poverty of materialism." Then, as time goes on, and Christianity is not accepted as a way of life, as a labor of total spiritual transfiguration, that same person can commit deeds that place him completely outside of Christianity. There lived a monk at the monastery of Valamo who did not want to recognize his own guilt, did not want to humble himself. Father John of Kronstadt appeared to him in a dream. "Dig deeper!" he said, "delve into the darkness of your heart until you find the golden nugget that enlightens it." So often one feels like telling our young ones, "Dig deeper!"

✠ ✠ ✠

"Monasticism in the world" or "white monasticism" is the affirmation of the narrow path of the Gospel for all, not only for a small group of people sheltered by the walls of a monastery. It is an effort to live the Christian life fully in the very swirl of daily concerns. In this sense it is a return to early Christianity. "Monasticism in the world" was not invented, it was brought into existence by the conditions of church history. Drawing to its end, history rediscovers its beginnings.

The world is returning to paganism; it has been moving in this direction for a long time. Now the process is speeding up and the great religious thinkers of recent times, Bishop

Tikhon of Zadonsk, Father Ambrose of Optino and Dostoyevsky speak more and more of monasticism in the world.

Love is a quality of will, or as Nicholas Cabasilas (14th
century) said, "a virtue of the will." All God wants from us
is this effort of will towards Him, our love for Him. He
reveals Himself to people not for their accomplishments and
deeds, as a kind of compensation, but only in response to the
love-will, to the desire to be with Him, to the will to live.
God is love and expects our love and waits for our will. Man
is entangled in his original sinfulness and can do nothing on
his own to find God, to reach his own salvation, except to
want and desire it, stretching his will towards it. God sees
this free will and helps man by the power of His grace. He
thus draws men closer to Himself and accomplishes all good
in their lives. Man does not accomplish good by his own
power, but by the power of divine grace which is drawn into
his life by his will and his love. Will and love express
themselves in effort and labor.

This is the basis of the church teaching that man is saved
freely, for the sake of his humble faith, not as a recompense.
Ascetic effort is merely an expression of our good will, of
our love for God. Spiritual labor is indispensable, but anything anyone achieves is not his own but God's and is gained
not by man's own effort, but by the grace of God. "Even if
we reach the summit of virtue, we are saved only by God's
mercy," says John Chrysostom. This is one of the most
remarkable and joyous contradictions of Christianity. It is a
joy to realize finally that you are nothing and that "everything is from Him, by Him and towards Him. Glory to Him
for ever!"

Man is cleansed of sin by the eternal light of God. This is accomplished not through man's merit, not through his ascetic efforts (although effort is indispensable) but "beyond reason," as a "holy mystery." The Holy Spirit gives life to every soul, it is "exalted in purity, illumined by the triune Unity in a sacred mystery" (4th Gradual Antiphon).

✠ ✠ ✠

We are separated from Christianity simply because at best, we are merely "natural" persons, and Saint Paul says "the 'natural' man does not receive the gifts of the Spirit of God" (1 Co 2:14). Yet there is a door through which we can enter the spiritual world of the Spirit of God: it is loving, prayerful, communion with our departed. We do not know how to be God-pleasing, but God is always accessible to love, and our love for our departed opens the door slightly into the world of the God of the living. That is the world where the departed are no longer dead but alive and loving, with God for eternity.

Blessed are our departed loved ones!

✠ ✠ ✠

Learning to know spirituality helps us to realize the relativity of time. The path to eternity "where there will be no more time" begins in spirituality. In the experience of spirituality the partitions and walls that separate our present from our past are taken down. Spirituality reunites us. We are reunited with our departed loved ones and our life with them, with our childhood and with treasures long lost.

Then something else, something new, becomes possible, changing one's past, changing one's own past self, as if one were washing away the dirty traces of our falls and betrayals. We are told, "All is possible to those who believe." I remember how Father Seraphim Batiugov used to say, "A time will come, in your inner life, when you will begin to heal your past."

In a prayer on the day of the Dormition we say, "The laws of nature are overcome in you, O all pure Virgin." God wants our salvation, and when God wishes, the laws of nature are overcome. Spirituality is that supernatural world, which a Christian must enter not "some day," "somewhere," but right here and now, on earth in the midst of modern civilization. Entering this spiritual world is itself an act of spirituality. Spirituality is the state of existence of any person who in some way tries to become part of the spiritual world. Spirituality is synonymous with the acquisition of godliness, because God is Spirit. Jesus calls God "Spirit" when he talks to Nicodemus (Jn 3:1–10) and discloses to him (and in his person to the entire human race) the reality of another divine world, and the difficulty of entering it. Spirituality is the Kingdom of the Divine Spirit. Christianity is a teaching about this kingdom and about how to enter it.

This is why the Gospel is permeated by the call "to seek the Kingdom of God." Nicodemus was awed and terrified as he realized the concept of new birth into spiritual life, and how supernatural this event is for human beings. We too are terrified by the very concept of spiritual life, and we try to camouflage its demands in philosophy, ecumenism, ritualism, in anything that will serve as a cover-up.

We should read the lives of the saints, but we must not limit our perception of a saint to the text of the book. We must try to learn something about him that may not be said in this record. Occasionally, the image of the saint, his individuality and the reality of his spiritual being, are clouded by a kind of pious "standardization." The miracle of a person's transfiguration, the "breath of Jesus" which each saint carries, remains unseen and unheard.

The "lives" of Saint Sergius of Radonezh, of Saint Seraphim of Sarov, remain unclouded, though they do contain many descriptions of miracles. This is why the image of Saint Seraphim is so close to us, so powerful. On a sunny summer day, I can look up and watch the clouds in the deep blue sky, and it is a joy for me to realize that similar clouds were moving in the blue sky above Sarov, and that Saint Seraphim may have been watching them. There is a new sense of discovery in this realization. I really live with him under the same undying blue sky of the Russian church.

✥ ✥ ✥

Terms like "virtue" and "piety," difficult to accept for intellectuals and young Christians today, acquire warmth and vitality in the experience of the reality of Church life. They become something unusual, but understandable. The word *podvig* (heroic feat) is a difficult one. And here are a few other examples: "Virtue is something so hot that it can set aflame our love for God and put our entire soul on fire" (Saint Nikita Stifat). "Piety is to visit orphans and widows in their affliction and to keep oneself unstained from the world" (Jm 1:27). "Passionlessness does not mean that you are not attacked by the spirits of evil, it means only that when they do attack you, they cannot conquer you" (The Righteous Diodochus).

✥ ✥ ✥

The closer we come to the end of our life, the stronger grows our love for the departed. Perhaps it is a premonition of our encounter with them? You think with joy not only of them, but of everything that is connected with them, their belongings, an old Gospel book, an armchair, a trail in the woods, the smell of hay, the sound of church bells. It seems as if nothing which somehow led a person of God ever dies.

"Everything comes from Him, is made by Him, leads toward Him." If "all things pre-exist in God," as Dionysius the Areopagite said, then everything that is good must exist, now and later and forever in God. We shall encounter everything again; all earthly warmth, purified and holy, will embrace us and we shall never be separated from it. We are approaching not a nirvana, but God's home, where we will find all those whom we had learned to love on earth.

5

Prayer and Fasting

Prayer is born of love. Is it not the same as to say, "Prayer is born of tears?" I realized this quite recently when I heard a young girl answer a question addressed to her. "How can I learn to pray?" The question did not puzzle her and she said unhesitatingly, "Go and learn to weep and you'll learn to pray." She completed the words of the Fathers.

✠ ✠ ✠

Modern city life leaves no place for lengthy prayers. Probably it is not a matter of incompatibility between our daily life and prayer. It is just that even in a Christian, believing home, it is difficult to isolate an hour of peace and quiet within the stream of daily cares, or to pray openly for any length of time. It seems that to withdraw into oneself for a length of time destroys something which is even more necessary than prayer in the modern desert of life. Thus anyone who lives in a close relationship with others must know the short prayer rule of Saint Seraphim of Sarov, teacher of Christian spirituality for modern times (the Lord's Prayer, Prayer to the Theotokos and The Creed). Saint Seraphim advises using the short prayer rule in the morning and then proceeding to one's daily work, constantly and silently appealing to God.

Bishop Theophan the Recluse also taught that any short

prayerful exclamation can serve as a morning prayer: "Lord, have mercy!" "Help me, O Lord!"

The real meaning of the new prayer rule is its brevity within the home and its constant use at work, among people. You must go out to people from your own private corner, but you must go with prayer in your heart.

✛ ✛ ✛

Bishop Theophan the Recluse used to say that praying only with words written by another is like trying to talk in a foreign language using only textbook dialogues. Like many other Church Fathers, he said that we must look for our own words in order to pray. I suppose that this is truly possible for us (if we dismiss artificially "invented" prayers of our own) only in moments of desperate need, real anguish, either for ourself or for others. In such moments we do not "recite" prayers, we simply cry out to God, "Lord, please come to him and comfort him!" The audacity of prayer is born only in the audacity of love. Saint Macarius said, "Love gives birth to prayer."

✛ ✛ ✛

"Love gives birth to prayer," therein lies the mystery and the meaning of prayer.

We can recite endless litanies, we can endlessly finger our prayer beads, but unless we have love, unless we have learned to grieve for others, we have not even begun to pray. We can thus go through all our life without having begun to pray. This is why Anthony the Great said, "Let's learn to love sorrow in order to find God!" He did not say "let us look for sorrow," but "let us love" it because sorrow is a cup offered us by Christ, and drinking it, we begin to partake of prayer.

Unless we are truly sympathetic to human suffering, we are merely carrying out a "prayer rule," not really praying.

To carry out a prayer rule is good and necessary, but only when we realize that it is a means, not an end in itself. We must realize that it is only a spur to encourage our efforts.

You cannot wait to be "in the mood" to pray; you have to use the spur of your prayer rule and force yourself to pray. A spur is nothing to boast about.

Imagine a man peacefully fishing from the shore. Everything is fine, everything is according to fishing rules, the brightly colored float gently bobs on the surface. The man does not realize that there is no baited hook attached to the line; the float is just a pretence, and actually there is no fishing taking place. To many people their prayer rule is such a baitless float; only the hook of suffering can catch real love.

✤ ✤ ✤

In one of his letters, Bishop Ignatius Brianchaninov wrote: "Regarding your private prayer rule, you must know that the rule exists for you. You do not exist for the rule, but live for the Lord. You must have the freedom of discernment."

✤ ✤ ✤

A friend of mine, a naval engineer who spent many hours every day working in a large office, used to say: "There is so much animosity, so much worry among all those people. I really did not know how to protect myself from it all. Then I decided to pray continuously while I work. Believe it or not, the results made themselves felt very soon. Not only did I gain peace of mind, but all the others who had dealings with me became more peaceful."

We know the words of Saint Seraphim of Sarov: "Acquire a peaceful spirit and many around you will be saved."

This young engineer friend of mine had a truly peaceful

spirit and his prayer was peaceful and humble. In Russian, the word "peace" (*mir*) and the word "humility" (*smirenie*) have the same root.

✢ ✢ ✢

Fasting means trying to overcome that which is "too human" in us. It means trying to overcome the limitations of our nature and to introduce it to limitlessness, to make it breathe eternity. Unfortunately, we pass on this heritage of the Church tradition to the young Christians of today in a somewhat distorted form, with a lack of true understanding.

Saint Maximus the Confessor said, "Ascetic labor, devoid of love, is unpleasing to God," yet this is the way fasting was usually practiced. There was a spirit of pride involved in one's own achievement and the effort remained outside of love. It often led not to a reduction but to an increase of hatred and coldness of heart.

✢ ✢ ✢

Everything in Christianity is determined and checked out by love. We should know some of the definitions of fasting given by saints:

Saint Isaac of Syria says: "Your spirit will not submit to the cross unless your body submits too" (This means effort, fasting).

Saint Paul writes: "You were called to freedom, brethren, only do not use your freedom as an opportunity for flesh" (Ga 5:13).

An elder said to his disciple whose fasting lacked love: "Eat everything, but do not eat people."

✢ ✢ ✢

Fasting must be understood, in the first place, as abstention from non-love, not from butter. Then it will become a time of light, a "joyous time of Lent."

> "Grant to my heart a pure fear of Thee, and to my soul perfect love."
>> (Stikhera to the hymn "Lord, I call upon Thee,"
>> 2nd, week of Great Lent)

Non-love, animosity, is the most terrible form of indulgence, a gluttony and intoxication with the self. It is the very first, the original offense against the Holy Spirit of God. "I appeal to you by the love of the Spirit" writes Saint Paul (Rm 15:30).

Love is the opposite of pride and hatred. In our evening prayers we ask forgiveness for those sins which are a breach of love.

> ... if I have reproached anyone, or become angered by something; or slandered anyone in my anger; or have lied or slept unnecessarily; or a beggar has come to me and I have despised him; or have saddened my brother or quarreled with him; or have judged someone or have allowed myself to be haughty, proud or angry ... or have laughed at my brother's sin ...

"Let me be free of all wrath ..." The other day I heard a young girl express very well the harmfulness of animosity towards other people. We were talking about life after death and she exclaimed, "But there we will have to meet each and everyone with joy!" Yes, we have to learn from the holy Fathers, but we must also learn from modern young girls.

✤ ✤ ✤

Few people know more about Khomyakov than that he was an officer in the imperial guards and then became the founder of a kind of "romantic theology." Here is a quotation from the little known memoirs of J F Samarin:

I was a guest at the Khomyakov country home. A number of us stayed overnight so that all the available rooms were full and my bed was placed in Khomyakov's own room. After supper, after endless conversations, brightened by his cheerful humor, we both lay down. I blew out the candle and fell asleep. Long after midnight I woke up. Dawn was just breaking. Without moving, without making a sound, I peered into the almost dark room. Khomyakov was on his knees, in front of an icon, his head leaning on his hands crossed on the back of a chair. I could hear him weeping quietly. This lasted for a long time, until daylight. Of course, I pretended that I was asleep and had heard nothing.

He joined us later in the day, just as cheerful as usual, full of pep, with his usual good-humored laugh. From a man who usually traveled with him, I heard that this happened almost every night.

✢ ✢ ✢

In a batch of old letters I recently found a letter written by a bishop to his spiritual daughter. He wrote, "If a sinner truly sighs once, feeling the burden of his sins, if just once he opens his heart to his Redeemer, the whole weight rolls away, all doubts disappear, his heart brims with faith and tears, and he feels so light and at ease." The last words are a quotation from a well known poem by Lermontov, but they were obviously so much a part of what the bishop felt, that he used no quotation marks. They were his words, and mine too, as well as anyone's who has experienced the grace of prayer which removes the weight of sin.

✢ ✢ ✢

"Pray constantly!" is a direct admonition of the Apostle. The Fathers of the Church teach us that only prayer of the heart can be constant. Our mind tires out, while the heart remains awake even when we sleep. For us, imperfect as we are, the most important element in the concept of constant prayer is sincerity. The Apostle demands from us constant, unwavering, prayerful sincerity in our relationship to God; he teaches us to exist in the sincere truthfulness of prayerful breathing.

If we understand prayer in this way, we cannot doubt that it is possible. There is no reason why sincerity should be impossible. I remember a story I heard from Metropolitan Kyril, whom I met in one of the camps. Before the Revolution, in one of the big Moscow railroad stations, there stood a splendidly uniformed door-keeper. Metropolitan Kyril said that this man was carrying on the spiritual labor of constant prayer for many years.

✤ ✤ ✤

I would like to think through the words of the Apostle calling us to constant prayer.

When we have completed our prayer rule, we pause after its completion, or after having attended a service of worship, we experience a kind of sense of achievement. The pauses are filled with self-satisfaction, by a feeling of enrichment from the recent experience of prayer and this state of mind is a denial of the very meaning of prayer. We have just said many times "Lord, have mercy!" and then, in the following pause, we feel satisfaction and fatigue and feel no need to beg for mercy. Interruptions in the experience of prayer can prepare a fertile soil for pride.

We are often victims of a kind of "post-prayer carelessness," "I have prayed, so everything is all right!" This opens the way to many temptations connected with prayer. The Fathers of the Church often speak of this.

There is a logic, a spiritual kind of logic, to constant prayer. Constant prayer serves to establish in us an absolutely sincere humility. I cannot not pray constantly, because I constantly need divine help. Why should I be proud of constantly calling for help? We do not feel pride because we breathe without interruption, we do not even notice it. We should not evaluate the process, we must just pray. Our prayer must acquire the unwitting simplicity of constant breathing.

Probably I will be criticized for writing thus. I am critical myself because I write about prayer without knowing how to pray. But I am quite sure of one thing, our sinful hearts should be at least filled with a yearning to pray. Yearning to pray is what a simple heart needs more than anything else.

✛ ✛ ✛

Theophan the Recluse wrote about prayer: "Our life is in our heart and that's where we have to love; do not think that this is a task for the perfect. No, this is how all search for God begins. We begin to love only when our heart grows warm with an unfailing constant warmth. This is the fire that our Lord brought down on earth."

"Unfailing constant warmth in our heart" is the grace of God which abides in us and which makes our heart simple and sincere. Father Nektary of Optino wrote, "Ask God for the gift of His grace. Pray simply, 'Lord grant me grace!'" You cannot gain grace by effort, but you can beg for it. In doing this we ask that our heart be simple, sincere, and warm. To pray for grace is like a person freezing in the cold, begging for warmth. "Come then, naked children of Adam, and let us clothe ourselves in Him, that we may warm ourselves" ("Ikos" for Epiphany).

✛ ✛ ✛

Prayer needs a certain quiet within us and around us. This is why it is so difficult to pray in our loud and arrogant days.

I remember a poem given me by G Chulkov, who later became a disciple of Father Alexei Mechev, and who was a friend of Alexander Blok:

I live in the worries of every day
But my heart, beneath their heavy weight,
Lives a life of its own,
Like a miracle of flame.

Hurrying to catch a bus,
Or bending over a book,
I can suddenly hear the murmur of fire
And I close my eyes.

Perhaps, in our days, prayer does live "under a heavy weight."

✣ ✣ ✣

One of the favorite prayers of Father Seraphim Batiugov was the Prayer to the Theotokos, "To thee, our leader in battle and defender, O Theotokos," in which we pray not for ourselves but for everyone. "In the terrible days we are living through" he said shortly before his death, "we must repeat it almost constantly."

And the nun Mary, who recently died in Zagorsk, after having been the spiritual counselor of many, also said that we must constantly pray to Mary, the Mother of God. They both meant the same thing—if we are to be saved, it is through the Theotokos.

✣ ✣ ✣

Our response to the closing down of churches must be an effort to maintain a constant remembrance of God. This would not only serve to get the churches reopened, but it is a way of building a temple that cannot be destroyed.

✣ ✣ ✣

The last words of Bishop Afanasy, in 1962, were, "You will all be saved by prayer."

A childhood recollection helps me to understand the words, "keeping the memory of God in one's heart." In the monastery I visited as a small boy, there was a chapel built over a well. On the inside of the roof there was an icon of Christ the Pantocrator. If I looked into the water, I could see in its dark, glassy surface a reflection of the icon. Thus, I believe, we can seen the image of Our Lord's blessing in the deep well of our heart.

We must remember the teaching of the Church Fathers: all good works can become a habit, but prayer always remains an unusual experience for us. How often we experience this quality of prayer, when with real effort we start the familiar routine of the morning prayer rule. The Church Fathers say that it is dangerous to interrupt prayer and that holding on to a rule is beneficial, a kind of spur. "The Kingdom of God is taken by violence," that is, we have to make an effort, we have to force ourselves. It is also said that the Kingdom of Heaven is within our heart. We have to take our heart in hand — a warm and firm hand — and then our prayer will take root.

Father Valentin Sventitsky taught that the constant prayer of the heart must continue even during church services.

"Love is greater than prayer," say the saints.

One year I was living in a small village, lost in the wilds. It was Holy Saturday, eve of the Resurrection of our Lord, but there was no church and no services that I could attend. I decided I would spend the night reading the Easter compline. Suddenly, there was a knock at the door, a lonely traveler was asking me to give him shelter for the night. I was quite upset, really indignant, "Can't I have even this one night for prayer?" I thought. Possessed by my irritation, I bundled him off to my neighbors and naturally, with him, off went my night of prayer and meditation. There are some sins we can never forgive ourselves. We must distinguish real prayer from the special kind of horrible and voluptuous devotions in which there is no love, and you are only conscious of your "self," reaching "heights of spirituality."

Turning away the traveler, having refused to take part in a meal of love, I rejected "sobornost," communion with him and with the Church as a whole. That Easter night, when I read the prescribed prayers, I was obviously outside of the communion of the Church.

The "agape," meals of love, were celebrated by early Christians together with the Eucharist. A Church Council in Carthage in 391 A.D. prescribed that the sacrament of Eucharist be celebrated separately and that Christians should fast before approaching the Holy Eucharist.

✛ ✛ ✛

"Sobornost" is the oneness of Christians in the holy Body of Christ. "Where two or three are together in My name, there am I in the midst of them" (Mt 18:20). "Sobornost" is the divine-human oneness of love, the Church. The Church is the gathering of Christ's disciples in "the temple of His body." "Let two become one."

6

Love and Humility

Christian renunciation of the world does not mean renouncing our love for it; on the contrary, it is a true affirmation of love for it. Quite consciously I say "love for the world," although if I used the words "love for people" I would avoid any seeming conflict with the words of the Apostle, "Do not love the world." People remember this quotation without really understanding it, yet there is another text that they neither remember nor understand, "God so loved the world ..." God loved, but we do not and thus we do not want to take part in what is said further, "God so loved the world that He gave His only Son" (Jn 3:16).

We condemn the world and are quite sure of our right to judge it, though in the very same Gospel passage we find the words, "God sent the Son into the world not to condemn the world, but that the world might be saved." Without love, how can we give ourselves up for people? Only the holiness of love can ascend to Golgotha.

Not to love the world means, first of all, not to love one's own darkness, one's own sinfulness, one's own selfhood and to realize that I am in this very dark and unloving world. Then, in this kind of "unlove" for the world, we begin to see the faint glimmering of our love for people and of a great compassion for the world.

✤ ✤ ✤

"Do not love the world" (1 Jn 2:15) ... "For God so loved the world ..." (Jn 3:16). What a remarkable contradiction in the Christian way of perceiving things, love and non-love, and it is expressed by the same Apostle, the Apostle of love.

Florensky explains the essence of this law of contradiction well, the law of antinomy. The contradiction is real, but it is resolved in a realistic fashion in the oneness of grace. Within the Church the human mind becomes part of this oneness.

Here is another example of contradiction, Saint Paul writes in his Epistle to Titus: "He saved us not because of deeds done by us in righteousness, but in virtue of His own mercy" (Ti 2:5-6). This truly sounds like the Lutheran teaching on salvation through faith alone, without any need of effort or good deeds. But just a verse later, Saint Paul adds, "so that justified by His grace ... those who have believed in God, may be careful to apply themselves to good deeds" (Ti 2:7-8). The "oneness" of these contradictions is truly the foundation of the holiness of Orthodox saints.

"Do not rely on your own self; all that is good within you is the product of God's grace and power" (Saint Abba Isaiah). This is the basic teaching of asceticism.

Another Saint wrote, "Exert effort ... and when you will be able to go beyond the realm of passionate desires, do not be ungrateful, refusing to recognize that this victory is a gift granted from above. Confess in the words of the Apostle, 'It was not I, but the grace of God which is with me'" (1 Co 15:11).

Father Nectary of Optino used to say, "Saint Mary of Egypt retired to the desert because of love," that is, love was the power behind her ascetic feats.

Monasticism is a true feat of love which was debilitated

a long time ago. This weakened spirit, a kind of reduction to formalism, was inherited by our modern Russian monastics. One really wonders sometimes, there is so much cold in our world, it is such a drafty place, yet we seem impelled to add more and more cold to it!

Recently I heard a young nun say, very confidently, that if an Orthodox Christian enters a Roman Catholic church he is thereby defiled. I thought, "O Lord Jesus, Thou Loving Warmth, have mercy on us."

And yet, among these very monastics, there suddenly appear, as a kind of miracle, real heroes of love, real disciples of Christ; and they, rather than the lay people, become bearers of light and leaders of men.

A person who cannot understand monasticism cannot understand early Christianity.

✠ ✠ ✠

Only once in my life did I experience the joy of generosity, yet there are many people whose hearts are generous throughout their life.

My experience took place in the Butyrky prison in the fall of 1922, and it was like a sunny wind that sweeps out all the dust and refuse accumulated in your heart. I was getting ready for my deportation and I distributed all my possessions. The more I gave away, the deeper I could breathe the air of freedom, that freedom to which we are called at all times. The short time of prison-born daring remained the happiest time of my life. Why did I not die then?

✠ ✠ ✠

There was another time. I stood at a huge window in a modern section of Moscow. It was night. Stars glimmered between the clouds like beacon lights. My heart was relieved of its burdens, as if I suddenly found the path I had lost in the surrounding darkness, the thread of life, woven from hope and joy. The huge city was no more alien to me, but an abode of suffering people.

We have not been embittered by those past fifty years and we pray for this city as one prays at the bed of a desperately sick person. This is the land of your people, O Lord!

✜ ✜ ✜

The simplicity and love to which we are called by the Apostle is surely not a simplification of things. It is bringing all our thoughts and feelings into a relationship of evangelical discipleship to Christ. Only this can help us find our way in the labyrinth of modern confusion.

Persons of Christian simplicity are "those who follow the Lamb wherever He goes ... in their mouth no lie was found ..." (Rv 14:4-5).

✜ ✜ ✜

According to the word of God, love is contrasted to lawlessness and intemperance, in other words to "non-holiness." "Because wickedness is multiplied, most men's love will grow cold" (Mt 24:13); "Do not use your freedom as an opportunity for the flesh, but through love be servants of one another" (Ga 5:13).

Christian holiness is love; lack of love is lack of holiness. The nature of love is unfathomable, because it is divine; but we do know one thing, if there is pride, there is no love. Love is a humble disregard of oneself, a giving up of oneself for others, for God, and for God's children.

Sin, on the other hand is "remembering oneself" and forgetting others. It is self-satisfaction, sometimes coarsely sensual, sometimes spiritually refined. Therefore all sins are, in a greater or lesser degree, a renunciation of love, a greater or lesser pride and conceit. "Make no provision for the flesh to gratify its desires" (Rm 13:14). Do not pamper yourself, do not become subjected to your own "selfness." Does not the same thing happen within our hearts, in our relationships with other people? Instead of giving ourselves to them, caring for them and being concerned for them, I remain absorbed in myself, I assert myself in my relations with them. In my communications with others I really watch myself, as in a mirror.

When I am at prayer, does it not happen that I really address myself? In this and in much more — when I judge others, when my feelings are hurt, when I am irritable, when I hate, when I greedily snatch at things — basically I am always doing the same thing. I assert myself, my own selfness, my ego, instead of the non-ego, instead of God and other people, instead of love.

On the other hand, after enumerating all the virtues to which we are called, the Apostle says, "and above all these put on love, which binds everything together in perfect harmony" (Col 3:14), for love is all that leads us to God. Love defeats pride, destroys selfishness and lust, both bodily and spiritual. Depravity can be caused by sin, but it can also be caused by false virtuousness. It can be caused by shift-lessness. but also by ascetic feats. The holy Fathers said, "better a defeat with humility than virtue with pride." True holiness and true love are one and the same. Saint Augustine also says, "Every virtue is love."

To recognize and truly experience this, some people have to live for many years, absorbing the words of the Fathers who teach us this shining way. This principle is the root of *askesis*, which is a struggle for love within yourself and in the whole world.

✠ ✠ ✠

Bishop Theophan the Recluse says, "The crux of the matter is that we must train our minds to live within our heart. Our mind must be transferred from our intellect into our feeling heart, the two must be made one ... " In other words, our thinking mind must become our loving mind. This is the depth and the warmth which the Church Fathers invite us to reach. Yet, in our very poor efforts to pray, our minds are immediately and firmly rooted in our own personal conceit and pride.

Macarius the Great used to say that our minds must be nailed to the cross of Christ.

✠ ✠ ✠

The Church Fathers have a great deal to say about how to save ourselves from sin, or, in other words, how to come closer to God. The way to God leads, through our attitude to other people, to our neighbors, and it is along this way too that spiritual death comes to us.

We can be angry at people, we can be proud in our relationships with them, or we can emanate sensuousness. Each one of these evil attitudes can bring us to our own spiritual death. We can also love a person, experience humility in our relationships and see someone with pure eyes. When this does take place, we suddenly discover that every human being is "an image not made by hands," which stands for Christ. Thus the practice of Christian life is reduced to having Christ stand between me and every other human being. We must see other people through Christ only.

✠ ✠ ✠

We have to speak of love and non-love, of holiness and non-holiness. This is the knot that holds together our spiritual existence.

Yet to speak of love means primarily to speak of humility, or more precisely, of humble love, because love does not seek its own, because love forgets "its own" and gives it up in humility. Only humility can forget about itself. Humility is the very essence of love, which gives up its own and sacrifices itself.

"To lay a foundation for love, we must begin by giving up ourselves," says the French military pilot Saint Exupery, speaking truly in the spirit of the Church Fathers.

Humility is a sacrifice. The best sacrifice is a broken spirit, "a heart broken and contrite, you have never disdained, O God" (Ps 51).

✥ ✥ ✥

In a letter dated in 1937 Father Seraphim Batiugov wrote thus about humility: "Humility is constant prayer, faith and hope, it is the love of a trembling heart which has given itself up to God. Humility is the door leading to our heart making it capable of experiencing spiritual life."

✥ ✥ ✥

Maybe the most difficult thing about humility is to accept humbly the non-love of others for us. Surely, we are justified in longing for this love, but we cannot demand it, even within our heart. For the commandment we have received is that we love others, not that we demand their love for us. The very essence of love is that we demand nothing for ourselves. Only when we achieve this non-demanding attitude does the golden bird of God's love come down into our heart and fill it.

✛ ✛ ✛

Father Valentin Sventitsky said to me once, "there we go, preaching about love and humility, but should anyone step on our toe in a crowded subway, we hate the offender ..."

Humility expressed in words only is born of pride, say the Church Fathers. Anyone who tries to think as a Christian says, without much difficulty, that he is "a great sinner" and even seems to experience pleasure in saying this. He may respond to a request for prayer by the standard verbal form, "My prayers are unworthy!" But try and say about your own self, quite sincerely, "I am no good!" "I am dirty!" and you will see how difficult it is.

I thought I was a humble man, yet Mother Smaradga said about me, just a few days before her death, "Sergei Iosifovich is spiritually proud." I stood convicted.

✛ ✛ ✛

Metropolitan Macarius used to say, "love is placed in us like a grain of seed" (Letters, 1915). We must try really to understand this. Love grows, gets stronger and more perfect, but its beginning is a small seed, and as a small seed it is present in a person's life from the very start. "Beginners" must possess it too.

All labor, all efforts, that do not originate from love and a humble spirit, are worthless (St Simeon the New Theologian). Does not the Gospel speak of that grain, too: "The kingdom of heaven is like a grain of mustard seed ... It is the smallest of seeds, but when it has grown, it is the greatest of shrubs ... so that birds of the air come and make nests in its branches" (Mt 13:31-32).

Did we not feel protected and safe in the perfect love of holy elders and some loving friends?

✠ ✠ ✠

"The beginning of pride is sin"
    (The Wisdom of Jesus Son of Sirach)

"Pride is self-love, self-appreciation and self-assertion. As love for God, which builds His city, is the origin and source of all virtues, thus love for oneself, of oneself, which moves us to build the tower of Babel, is the source of all sins."
    (Saint Augustine, *The City of God*).

"Love is the root and birthgiver of all that is good" (St John Chrysostom). All defects are the results of pride, all the virtues result from humility and love.

7

Suffering

We have to understand and to accept that Christianity is not a kind of rational social teaching that can solve all the problems of the human community. Christianity cannot be identified with humanism. According to the words of Christ it is not "peace, but a sword." It calls us to overcome not social injustice but human nature, in order to transfigure it into divine nature. Christianity is the transfiguration of man into God through the communion of divine grace. Such a sublime goal explains the need for "the narrow way," for "asceticism," for spiritual heroism, for the "sword" of Christianity. Only in the suffering of Golgotha can God be born in man.

The suffering of Golgotha is greater than human nature, so much greater that Christ Himself prayed for it not to happen. He prayed in agony and His sweat fell like drops of blood. It is no easy matter to graft a taste for eternity onto human nature, yet this is the very purpose of Christian faith, the deification of man, the whole man, soul and body. If the suffering of Golgotha, "the narrow way," is renounced, this renunciation deprives Christianity of its deepest meaning. Such "sterilized Christianity" becomes merely one of the numerous groups whose members are concerned with social problems. Father Seraphim Batiugov told me once: "Christianity is not a poem; it is a heroic achievement, a 'podvig'."

✤ ✤ ✤

We find the term "deification" embarassing. The horizons it opens before us are too overwhelming. Yet it is only through this window that we can see Christianity as a whole, "the love of Christ in its whole breath and depth, beyond all understanding," which makes us not only the royal priesthood but also gods according to grace. "By his divine blood Christ redeemed mortal man subjected to the tyrant-loving sin, and, making him like unto God, He renewed him. For He hath been glorified" (Canon of the Resurrection, Tone 3, Canticle 1).

✤ ✤ ✤

The other day I came across a wonderful sentence in the writings of the Church Fathers: "To help them bear their sufferings, the holy martyrs were given a special grace, not only spiritually, but bodily too." This means that their physical, material body was made holy while they were still alive. Their bodies suffered and became exhausted, but they were already invincible. In Christian experience human flesh becomes illumined by the light of eternity during its existence here. It is illumined by the divine-human flesh of Jesus Christ. "For our sake, Christ, Who is God, was united to the flesh and crucified and died, was buried and rose again, and with His own flesh went up in light to the Father, and with it He shall come and save those who piously serve the same" (Canon to the Cross and Resurrection, Canticle 5, Tone 1). This is the abysmal difference between Christianity and spiritualistic philosophies.

In Christianity we find a living sense of the providential, non-accidental unity of each particular soul with each particular body. This unity is temporarily interrupted by death, but is reestablished in resurrection. The holy Fathers teach us that even after death our soul somehow bears the image of the body and remembers it. Saint Iraeneus of Lyons says, "Human souls have the image of man, they can be recognized and they remember their earthly existence" (*Against Heresies*, Book 2, chapter 34). The human soul loves its body, its temple, with a divine love.

✛ ✛ ✛

For Christians the feat (*podvig*) of living is unavoidably linked to some kind of suffering within the measure of their strength. The suffering of Christians is similar to birth pains, it is a painful process bringing the sufferer to a joyful end (Jn 16:21).

This is a test of our Christianity, are we giving birth to that child of joy? "For as we share abundantly in Christ's sufferings, so in comfort too" (2 Co 1:5).

It is always a dangerous symptom when we begin to complain, when we become embittered and grumble at every pretext. If not joyful, we should be at least good-humored, if not good-humored, we should at least have a sense of humor in regard to our troubles, temptations and battles. Our attitude of sophisticated intellectual exhaustion is a kind of refusal to bear our cross. Christ commends the early Christian Church saying: "I know you are enduring patiently and bearing up for my name's sake, and you have not grown weary" (Rv 2:3).

✛ ✛ ✛

"When the soldiers mocked Thee, O Lord, before Thy death upon the precious cross, the heavenly hosts were struck with wonder. For Thou, who hast adorned the earth with flowers wast arrayed in a crown of shame; and Thou who hast wrapped the firmament in clouds, wast clothed in a robe of mockery. Thus, in Thy providence, O Christ, Thou hast made known Thy compassion and great mercy, glory be to Thee" (Great and Holy Friday, Troparion of the third hour).

According to the Apostle we are "heirs of God and fellow heirs with Christ, provided we suffer with Him in order that we may also be glorified with him" (Rm 8:17). "Provided"...If only! Suffering is accepted in Christianity as a means of "ascending to God." The one who wants to be a Christian must discover in his heart a warm pain, a life-giving wound by which he takes part in the life and suffering of Christ and of all people.

This is why we are called to pray daily, "with Thy love wound our heart" (sixth hour). Christians live with an open wound.

✠ ✠ ✠

Father Alexander Elchaninov said, "The meaning of suffering is to participate in the suffering of Jesus Christ and in the creation of the Body of Christ on earth." This is why Church Fathers called the building of our salvation a "build-ing of suffering."

The frightening phenomenon of our days is that the world is plunged into an ever-deepening abyss of actual suffering, and at the same time the very concept of suffering becomes more and more hateful to people. From the Christian point of view an opposite correlation is better.

In Christian experience suffering is twofold. First is is an act of compassion, "suffering with," or love which is almost co-existence. A man co-suffers with his crucified God and through Him co-suffers with all men and all the suffering earth. This suffering is unavoidable and every Christian must experience it within the measure of his love. The other sort of suffering is a kind of "heroic feat" ("podvig"). Quite often it does not actually involve pain because our Lord bears it for us, seeing our yearning for Him. The Church Fathers teach that some people attain salvation without painful effort, only through humility and love. We must remember the words of Saint Augustine, "where there is love, there is no suffering, and even if there is suffering, you love it."

✣ ✣ ✣

"Sorrow is the food for love. Love that is not nurtured by sorrow, in however slight a quantity, shrivels and dies, like a new-born infant whom we would try to nurture with adult food. Yes, it is necessary for love to shed tears. Very often, at the very moment when we shed tears, our love is forged and tempered into shape" (Maurice Maeterlink, *Treasure of the Humble*).

Father Golubtsov used to say, "Many saints saw angels weeping."

✣ ✣ ✣

In some of the very early Christian apocrypha, which did not become part of the New Testament, we find words ascribed to Christ: "He who stands close to Me, stands close to fire; he who is far from Me, is far from the Kingdom" (Origen, *Comments on Jeremiah 20:8*; Didymus, *Commentary on Psalm 7:8*; *Gospel according to Saint Thomas*, discovered in 1941).

Christianity sears human thinking with the experience of suffering, and God cannot be born in man without the presence of flame.

Today, not only does the secular world hate the idea of suffering, but this hatred is shared by those who call themselves Christians and are active churchmen. Hatred of suffering creates a false Christianity, a kind of Christian atheism.

✛ ✛ ✛

The dogma of Christ's humanity opens up to us the ineffable self-impoverishment of God, the suffering of God. It is as indispensable as the dogma of Christ's divinity, but reading books on the subject is of no help. Come to church on the eve of Great Saturday, listen to the chanting of the praises, and this experience will be more meaningful: "The cause of life willingly endures death, desiring to quicken life ... One of the Trinity, for our sake suffering in flesh a shameful death ... My Christ, the invisible light, hidden in the tomb and deprived of life ... The angels are puzzled and amazed, shouting: 'How is the treasure of life seen dead?!' "

✛ ✛ ✛

It seems to me that if, in the Nicene Creed, the words "suffered and was buried and rose again ..." were replaced by the words "suffered and died and rose again ...," the reality of the incarnation would have been expressed with more strength. He arose on the third day, not in His divinity, which had never died, but in his humanity, thus the words "arose" and "suffered" do convey the reality of His incarnation. But in the Scriptures and in the writings of Church Fathers, the death of Jesus Christ is emphasized and I believe it is done so in order to have the divinity of Jesus Christ shine even more brilliantly at this ultimate point of His humanity. The word "buried" only relates a fact, but does not explain a doctrinal truth. There are also other great facts in the life of our Savior which are not mentioned in the Nicene Creed — Epiphany, Transfiguration and other events.

"Is it Christ Jesus, who died, yes, who was raised from the dead ... " (Rm 8:34).

"And He died for all, that those who live might live no longer for themselves, but for Him who for their sake died and was raised" (1 Co 5:15).

"... Jesus Christ, the faithful witness, the firstborn of the dead ..." (Rv 1:5).

The closer man — and our whole world — comes to the experience of Golgotha, the more we need to understand the revelation of Christ's death, inseparable from His resurrection. The better we understand the humanity of Jesus in the light of His divinity, the more reassured and certain we feel, because we, too, "... carry in the body the death of Jesus so that the life of Jesus may also be manifested in our bodies" (2 Co 4:10). "I am the first and the last and the living one; I died and behold I am alive for evermore" (Rv 1:17-18).

I do not understand the suffering of the world. I only understand that the Creator of the world became part of the world's suffering and let His beloved Son share in it. Christianity speaks to us of God who suffers, suffers not because of His guilt, but because of compassion, because of love. If this is so, then suffering is not to be feared, because it cannot be separated from love, or from God. "God suffers in His flesh ..." That is why we dare to say "Of Thy sufferings make me a participant" (Stikhera on "Lord, I call upon Thee," Tuesday, 2nd week of Great Lent).

8

Thinking About God — The Theology of Our Days

The Fathers of the Church taught that prayer is theology and theology is prayer. Practically, we must understand this to mean that only a theology which is a bridge to prayer is necessary for those who approach the walls of the Church.

After all the mathematics of Father Florensky, it is easy to begin to pray. He almost never wrote about prayer, but he was building a fragrant temple for it. His metaphysics are always full of nostalgia for the homey churches of Old Russia.

I get the same kind of impression from the theological writings of Metropolitan Anthony (Bloom). Some other contemporary theologians are penetrated by a kind of religious rationalism, whether gnostic, philosophical, or Orthodox. Through their many words, you cannot hear silence, yet this theological silence is more important than anything else.

✠ ✠ ✠

"I decided to know nothing among you, except Jesus Christ and Him crucified," wrote Saint Paul (1 Co 2:2). This is the center from which radiate the theological teachings of the apostles, like waves created by a stone dropped into water.

I remember a very ancient icon I saw once, an image of the Savior called "Jesus the Gracious Silence." Our Lord was represented as the "Angel of Great Council," as the focus of all Divine wisdom and knowledge.

Sight and knowledge inspired by grace, this is the very air the Church breathes. If we are within the Church, if we love, then we also know and theologize, for love gives birth to knowledge of the Church. Members of the Church can, and some of them indeed do, nourish their minds with general knowledge and science, but their hearts and minds must live so as to "know nothing except Jesus Christ and Him crucified."

✠ ✠ ✠

Saint Barsanuphius, an ascetic of the fourth century, tells us how general human knowledge, or "worldly wisdom," can be harmonized with divine wisdom: "You must not pay attention to worldly wisdom only, for if you are not granted spiritual wisdom from above, all wisdom is vain. Blessed is the one who has both worldly and spiritual wisdom." How few are these blessed ones!

✠ ✠ ✠

There are many poets today whose poems are technically more perfect than Pushkin's or Blok's. Yet we all know that we have no poets like Pushkin or Blok today.

The same could be said about theology. There are many people today who, theologically speaking, are quite literate and can speak intelligently, professionally, and quite fearlessly about "gnosis," "asceticism," "energies," "transfiguration," "sobornost," "cataphatic and apophatic tradition." All the words seem to be correctly used, but listening to them is tedious and wearisome. Theology can become dinner-table talk, while it should be part of a feast of prayer and of the simplicity of love.

"Reading fine investigations about God dries out our tears and destroys the tenderness of our heart" (*Paterik*). "Seek God, but to not try to discover His abode" (Saint Seraphim of Sarov).

✠ ✠ ✠

The religious insights of such authors as Dostoyevsky or Pasternak were granted them by God to make up for the religious barrenness of the literature of their time. They were as a kind of compensation and can be compared to the voice of Balaam's ass, which put a stop to the prophet's delusion.

It is interesting to note that the religious value of world literature is rooted not in rationalistic theological reasoning but in the truly inspired writings of the Church. For example, ancient hermits encouraged their disciples to memorize passages from the New Testament and the Psalms. I am sure the American writer Ray Bradbury knew nothing of this tradition, but he makes the last people living after the destruction of our civilization memorize chapters from the Gospels (*Fahrenheit 451*).

I think that this advice of the Church Fathers and of a modern novelist should be taken to heart by all of us. We can memorize favorite passages from the New Testament and make them part of our prayer rule.

✠ ✠ ✠

Gogol published his pious letters with the best of intentions, but the elders of Optino Monastery were very critical of them. The *Summa Theologica* of Saint Thomas Aquinas is considered to be the foundation of Catholic theology, yet Berdyaev said, "Had I read the whole of it, I might have lost all faith!"

On the other hand, some poems of Lermontov, Tiutchev, Pasternak, Blok and others can bring us closer to faith and strengthen it. I knew a man who spent a year in solitary confinement in prison and had only one book to read, a volume of Dostoyevsky. He had been an atheist, but during that one year he found faith.

What conclusions can we draw from all this? We must be wise as serpents and meek as doves. Our literature is full of chaos and depravity. There are many books that simply should not be read because they are harmful, but we must not deny that a light may be suddenly perceived in this dark forest. If all people can be "God's people," so can their poems and their writings. Everything is from Him, by Him, towards Him. As Saint Paul says, quoting a pagan poem, "In Him we live and move and have being" (Ac 17:28).

In the crush of the rush hour subway I sometimes pray to my Guardian Angel in the words of Tiutchev's poem:

Shelter me with thy wing
Calm my restless mind.
Gracious will be thy shade
For my becalmed soul.

I purposely mentioned Gogol's pious writings, for some of our young Christian converts tend to accept uncritically all the pre-revolutionary church publications. This is a mistake which is dangerous for our spiritual health. All the evils we see within the church today — indifference to the individual, attaching great importance to the externals of prayer and asceticism (whatever there is of it), obliterating the dividing line between church and state, secularization, life according to the needs of our flesh and not to God's spirit — all this is the inheritance we received from our past. My father was a devoted priest, a disciple of the Optino elders, but I remember well how he suffered in the stifling, pre-thunderstorm atmosphere of church life in his day. I think it is symptomatic that the Church excommunicated Leo Tolstoy, but said nothing about Rasputin, who even found protection at a very high level of the church hierarchy.

✤ ✤ ✤

Converts often ask what they should read to strengthen their faith. As far as Christian faith is concerned, only one book fully discloses it, the New Testament. All other books attain this only to a certain degree. We must never accept unconditionally, totally, any other book, even when it proclaims Christian faith. The writings of Saint Basanuphius the Great, for example, are very close to those of Saint Paul, and great is the spiritual power of Church Fathers. But there are many books, with the most Orthodox titles, probably written with the best intentions, which blur the meaning of Christianity and even distort it.

"The word of God is living and active, sharper than a two-edged sword," said Saint Paul (Hebrews 4:12). Only such a sword can slice through the entanglements and the obscurity of dogmatic and pseudochurch literature. It shows us the way as clearly as a ray of light. Yet reading the Word of God is an exertion, an effort. You can read Rosanov or Thomas Aquinas, or perhaps even Vladimir Solovyev, while enjoying a cigarette, but not Saint Paul or Saint Macarius the Great.

✤ ✤ ✤

There is a theology that we might call "school theology," we can even speak of a "drawing room theology," but there also exists the true wonder and amazement of "thoughts about God," which is a joyous theology. This was the theology of Father Paul Florensky who was also a very learned theologian. A friend of his said once that "Florensky's greatness was not his learnedness, but the fact that he knew how to overcome his learnedness." You could sense this every time you came in touch with him, for in his serenity there was always a breath of truly spiritual, logical reasoning. Why do I mention "reasoning" only? Because the spiritualization of man, as a whole being, of his soul and body, begins with the reasoning mind. At sunrise, light reaches first the hilltops only, while the rest is still in shadow.

I remember seeing Florensky, in the summer of 1917, talking to his friends, Sergius Bulgakov and the painter Nesterov, at his home in Zagorsk. At that time Nesterov was painting the portrait called "The Two Philosophers." It was such a lovely, clear, cool summer morning. It seemed to us that new opportunities were being opened up for the Church, opportunities to become free of secularism and of submission to the State. But this freedom and independence had to be paid for by sacrifices and suffering so great that many proved unable to bear them.

Theosophy is not as harmless as it may seem. It refuses to recognize the Church as God's physical presence in the world, as "God's Body." The reality of this presence is unbearable for the dark and abstract thinking of spiritualism.

The Church is the Body of God. This inconceivable fact is perceived in the life-experience of each Christian through attaining a growing godliness of soul and body, through the labor of transfiguration. It is each particular soul and body, my own and your own, that become godly; and the responsiblity for this is laid upon each particular. In Christianity, there is no mist of endless rebirths to free us from responsibility. The Church accepts each particular human being and leads him or her into eternity, making of the person a cell of the Great Body. Human physical existence becomes part of eternal life.

✢ ✢ ✢

A person is not untrue to his Orthodox faith or to his piety if he comes to recognize a mistake or an error made by a saint. But he will be untrue to his Orthodoxy if he starts looking for such errors, consciously searching them out.

Saint Barsanuphius says quite simply that saints make mistakes. What is so terrible about that? In his Epistle to the Galatians (ch 2), Paul speaks of Peter's error in Christian doctrine in the matter of circumcision.

Very often it is not a matter of error, but a matter of a language, of speaking in a way that has become unfamiliar to us. Saint John Chrysostom spoke in the rhetorical style of fourth century Byzantium, which to us seems heavy, useless and even irritating. Father Seraphim Batiugov said it is almost impossible for a modern reader to read Saint John Chrysostom; his works must be published in a different form.

At the same time Saint John Chrysostom is vitally necessary to us and easily accessible through his Divine Liturgy, through his prayer before Holy Communion, through his Easter sermon. These works are like ships, carriers of his sublime thought, that have reached us over seas of rhetoric, "Grace shining forth from your lips like a beacon, has enlightened the universe ..." (Troparion to Saint John Chrysostom).

Christians believe in miracles, but always in terms of human existence, not in terms of history. Christianity does not shift historical events and history. There is nothing heretical in not believing that Saint Luke painted a venerated icon of the Theotokos in an elaborate Byzantine style of the 11th or 12th century. Such a belief is not obligatory for us, yet we will fail in our Orthodox consciousness if, looking at the ancient "Vladimir" icon of the Theotokos, we will fail to realize how close it is to the Gospel image of Mary, even though it is painted by a medieval Byzantine artist. The icon could not have been painted by the Evangelist, for this is historically impossible, but it carries the apostolic vision of divine truth. As Metropolitan Anthony Bloom said in 1966, "An icon is a vision of the world to come."

✛ ✛ ✛

I had read 500 pages of Thomas Aquinas and, to me, they seemed like a great desert. Suddenly I came across words that were truly alive. "Man realizes his faith through an act of his heart."

A simple nun, who knew nothing of Thomas Aquinas, lived in great poverty and constant hard work. One day she saw that she had no more tea left and was greatly distressed. She turned to the icon of the Theotokos and said, "Mother, you see, I have no more tea!" These words were an act of the heart, they came from the heart's daring.

✛ ✛ ✛

Divine grace acts in man's freedom, and freedom acts in grace. As Bishop Theophan the Recluse said, "they are mutually interpenetrating." Thus the process of salvation of each man takes place through the invisible action of both powers, grace and freedom.

✛ ✛ ✛

Man's freedom expresses itself in his own movement towards God. Because of the sinfulness of his nature, this movement is always a struggle, an ascetic effort to save the self from sin. All ascetic effort is an act of human freedom, a free choice to come closer to God. If freedom and divine grace are mutually "interpenetrating" and inseparable, then slothfulness and weakening of effort result in a reduction of divine presence. Divine grace and its gifts in the life of an individual are manifested not by some kind of document or certificate, but by the holy fire living in him.

One can have a certificate that divine grace was granted to him at some time in life, but it may no longer be present. Saint Paul writes, "Rekindle the gift of God that is within you through the laying on of my hands" (2 Tm 1:6).

Our anxieties for young Christians are, of course, justified. Sometimes they accept too blindly the entire heritage of our confused and confusing church history without distinguishing the inner meaning from external forms—the basic, unconditional truths, from that which is conventional. Sometimes they accept Christianity as if it were a very intelligent philosophical theory, not as the difficult way of Church life which they must follow and in which they have to share.

But we must not exaggerate our fears. We can see that divine grace itself teaches people today and leads them on. Sometimes I am amazed to see a person who only recently learned about Christianity speak of it and understand it better and at a deeper level than such an expert as Vladimir Solovyev.

God knows His chosen ones!

The Soviet daily newspaper *Izvestia* printed the following report (June 26, 1969):

"Speaking of the modernist trends in the Anglican Church,

Archbishop Basil of the Russian Orthodox Church, calls it 'Christian atheism.' He says that this new religious movement denies the very foundation of Christian faith — belief in a personal God, Creator and Provider, belief in the divinity of Jesus Christ, in His resurrection and in the life to come."

Christian atheism is based on the denial of Christianity as a miracle. It is a kind of turning off from the road to eternity and taking a road to earthly comfort. It is very easy to turn the effort aimed at the transfiguration of human nature by divine grace into an effort of overcoming the earthly ills of humanity, and to replace Christ's Golgotha by scientific and social concerns. But this will not be Christian faith, it will be disbelief in Christianity.

Is it a matter that concerns Anglicans only? Maybe, within Anglicanism, open doubts about dogmas of faith are admissible. Yet it is quite possible, without openly rejecting dogmas, inwardly to disbelieve them and to live as if they did not exist. The dogma of Christ's bodily resurrection becomes part of a person's theology only when he or she personally participates in Christ's resurrection through his own personal Golgotha, when death and resurrection are a personal experience. Is it not the beginning of "Christian atheism" when there is an inner disbelief in dogmas, even when the dogmatic exterior is preserved? Perhaps Christian atheism is only the last stage of an ancient and general process of the secularization of the Church?

Defenders of such pseudo-Christianity call old-fashioned believers — those who believe like the apostles did — "traditionalists," "defenders of archaic Christianity." When I read this, my heart is filled with bitter sorrow, "O Lord, why have I lived so long?" A poem by Pasternak comes to my mind, where he described his vision of Transfiguration. I also remember a poem describing Pasternak's funeral:

> There was a crowd of them,
> walking singly and in twos.
> Suddenly someone said:
> It's August 6th today —
> The Transfiguration of Our Lord
>
> On that day on Mount Tabor
> A Flameless light appears,
> and our eyes are drawn
> To autumn, limpid as a sign.

Eschatology, an apocalyptic vision of the world, is so close to the Russian heart that it can sometimes serve as a camouflage for spiritual indolence and egoism. "Since everything is so bad, and the end of the world is imminent, I'll just take care of my own salvation." Dostoyevsky called such an attitude "living for one's spiritual belly."

Early Christianity left us a special antidote for this sickness. It is a belief (and it has never been condemned by the Church Councils) that there may be a "first resurrection" described in the mysterious 20th chapter of the Book of Revelation, i.e., a kind of triumph of Christianity on earth. If Christianity can triumph on earth; even within the limits of the Church, which does not include all humanity, and for a limited period of history (symbolically called "one thousand years"), then it means that each one of us must somehow take part in this hope and must work towards its fulfillment. If we try sincerely and with an open mind to comprehend the meaning of the words "Thy will be done — on earth as it is done in Heaven," it is clear that we cannot isolate ourselves from the rest of the world and its concerns, whether the early Christians were right or wrong in their interpretation of the Book of Revelation.

We must somehow experience a concern for our earth, a yearning for God's righteousness to be established here, in our personal and our social life, in science, in art, whether we can achieve it or not. It is not a dogma of faith, but a yearning, a prayer.

Archimandrite Theodore Bukharev said, "In the person of Christ is contained everything human. Therefore, everything can be the object of your research, study and participation, but it must be done in the light of Christ and your soul must be directed to Him, Who took upon Himself all that is human."

A Christian understanding of history is as important as Christian faith in general. Our hope for the realization of God's truth (righteousness) on earth can be achieved only at the cost of a heroic effort to overcome the perishable nature of man. We have to come out of the limitations of our human nature, we have to go beyond its dimensions, into the dimensions of angelic life, out of the coldness of human relationships into the original warmth of divine life.

In terms of human history this is unimaginable for us sinners, and if this "millennium of the saints' reign" ever takes place, it will be beyond our historical framework and will be a kind of preparatory step into life eternal. St Irenaeus of Lyons speaks of such a preparation of the Church by means of a "millennium kingdom." It must be understood in terms of eschatology, above and beyond our historical concepts. The coming of such a "millennium" is possible only as a miracle of grace, not as the result of an organized Christian effort and scientific labor as proposed by Teilhard de Chardin.

Our yearning for a happy earth is part of our faith in a New Earth and New Heaven ...

When we come across a distortion of Christianity, a heresy, a schism, we must remember that such distortions may originate as a reaction against an already existing distortion in the life of the Church. Arianism (a reduction of the divine nature of Christ) is a reaction against a diminution of His humanity, against the fact that Christians tend to forget the reality of the suffering Son of Man. The result of this distorted image of Christ is a nebulous, painless theory which does not impose any sense of responsibility. Wrestling against Arianism, we must look for its cause, its antipode within our non-Arian environment, and struggle against it too.

Whatever we do, however zealously we fast or theologize, if we do it outside the light of Golgotha, we remain outside the Church. "He who does not love, remains in death" (1 Jn 3:14). Thus, as long as he does not love, he is not within the Church, because the Church of the living God and death cannot be one.

Metropolitan Anthony Bloom writes, "Where there is no love, there is no Church. There remains only its external form, a deceit, which repulses people. That is why our churches remain empty, that is why our young people lapse. Lord, help us to become your Church, not only its appearance" (Sermon on the healing of the paralytic). The Church was made possible by what took place on Golgotha. This is the price of the Church and only by paying that price can we enter it.

Bishop Theophan the Recluse says, "The crux of the matter is that we must train our mind to live within our heart. Our mind must be transferred from our intellect into our feeling heart, the two must be made one ..." In other words, our thinking mind must become our loving mind. This is the depth and the warmth which the Church Fathers invite us to reach. Yet in our very poor efforts to pray, our minds are immediately and firmly rooted in our own personal conceit and pride.

Macarius the Great used to say that our minds must be nailed to the cross of Christ.

9

Christians Outside the Orthodox Church

Quite recently an Orthodox priest, who willingly lent religious books to a college student, learned suddenly that the young man had joined the "Adventists." The priest said, "Our friendship is over, you are now in the enemy camp. I will give you no more books!"

The sectarians feel the same way about us. They think that "we adore graven images" because we venerate icons. They call themselves "believers," presupposing that we are "unbelievers."

Somewhere, way up above us and them, learned people make well-meaning speeches and attend international ecumenical conferences, but the multi-million masses, calling on the name of Christ, remain in the age-old darkness of estrangement and suspicious enmity. For all practical purposes the ecumenical movement of modern times has not healed the confessional splits in the minds of the people.

I am conscious of this antagonism within myself. I feel exasperated when people turn away from the icon of Our Lady of Vladimir and do not notice the expression of her eyes. I am exasperated when they refuse to recognize the revelation in Rublev's icon of the Holy Trinity, when they refuse to recognize that this divine serenity is what the

Church means — not what "I" am, or "he" is. Icons express something that is above human sinfulness, which corrupts all people in all religious associations without exception.

Yet sometimes I feel that Protestant sects have something of the primitive Christian Church and that some day their lack of understanding of what the Church is will come to an end. This is how I understand the words in the Book of Revelation: "The dragon was angry with the woman (that is, with the Church) and went off to make war on the rest of her offspring, on those who keep the commandments of God and bear testimony to Jesus" (Rv 12:17). If those "others" keep the commandments of God and bear testimony to Jesus, then truly it is a great and shattering achievement against the background of all that happens in the world today.

In the Creed, immediately after the words "I believe in one holy, catholic, and apostolic Church," we say "and in one baptism." Why "one Church" and "one baptism?" In the early centuries of Christianity there were many arguments about whether to re-baptize those who had lapsed into heresies and then returned. It was finally agreed that baptism, correctly performed, could not be repeated, for the grace it conveyed remained with the Christian, even if he later erred. Today, too, the Church does not re-baptize sectarians who have been baptized in their heretical community. Baptism is the door through which one enters the Church. Then, if a member of a sect is not re-baptized, does it not mean that, in a mysterious way, he has already passed through this door and, being a member of his sect, he still is in union with the Church? This probably supports Khomyakov's theory about the mystical ties of the Church with all "other" Christians in the world. For many Roman

Catholics and Orthodox the Church is identified with the clergy. According to the letter of the Eastern Patriarchs of 1848, the Church is the Orthodox people. Maybe, after our death, we will come to see that the boundaries of the Church are even wider.

✤ ✤ ✤

Archimandrite Theodore (Bukharev) believed that the basic error of Roman Catholicism consists not in their belief in the supreme authority of the Pope, but in the non-recognition of the supreme authority of Christ. Christ is the reality of the passion of Golgotha and of the resurrection of each individual person believing in Him. Christ means the supernatural transfiguration of a person here and now. But men and the Church, or rather church leaders, are scared by the tremendous task and try to restrict it to something that does not impose on us anything as terrible as this, does not involve the thorns of Golgotha. Superficiality does not impose such thorns whether it be an external kind of ecumenism, external ritualism, or deadly lawfulness, i.e., a belief that one can be saved by one's own good acts, or a blind submission to hierarchical authority, or even a naive Byzantine predilection for an order of rules ("typicon").

In all these ways we digress from the simplicity of Christ, from His supremacy. Observing the course of events, we see that Orthodoxy and many Orthodox Christians are full of such digressions.

This is the true cause of church divisions and this is the real reason we seem to be unable to come together again. In order to reunite all of us again, we and they must return to the acknowledgement of the supremacy of Christ.

10

Saints and Sinners of Our Times

A person is holy when he is filled with the grace of God. We do not understand clearly what "fullness of grace" means, and thus there is no more abstract and mysterious concept in modern church piety than the concept of holiness. Real holiness is replaced in church life by its semantics, the title we give it. It is one of the symptoms of the hardening of Christianity in history. The Church is suffering the old and terrible disease of secularization. Yet, we still know that the Church lives and is holy. It is holy not only in its sacraments but in the real holiness of its saints (many of them still unknown), in the loving faith of simple hearts.

Vladimir Soloukhin looks for icon "black boards" to discover beauty under the blackness. We do not look for anything special, but God grants us encounters with living icons, God's people.

✤ ✤ ✤

Mother Smaragda was an old blind nun who lived near the city of Voronezh and who died quite recently. I know that she practiced constant prayer and that she had the gift of foresight. However, today I want to tell something about another aspect of her life.

In the little town where Mother Smaragda lived, there was a young homeless beggarwoman of ill repute. Mother

Smaragda lived with another nun in a tiny cell. They were sorry for the waif, took her in and cared for her for two years. Then, suddenly, she left them, leaving behind disorder, dirt and her lice-infested rags. Months passed and Mother Smaragda met her again, this time in the market place, homeless, penniless and in rags, sitting on the ground with a newborn infant in her lap. Smaragda, probably with an inner sigh of regret for the quiet and cleanliness of her cell that she saw disappearing again, said to the other nun, "Dashka, we're Christians, aren't we? Let's take her in." And they took the tramp in, and the baby too, of course, and cared for them.

Mother Smaragda attended services in a church where she knew the priest to be an unbeliever. This was a real trial for her, but she had no choice; there was no other functioning church within reachable distance. When she went to confession, she would confess her sins standing before the icon of Saint Spiridon, for whom she had a special devotion, then she went to make her confession before the priest. Going to confession to the priest was important as an example of humility and of the inadmissibility of splits in the Church. Once she told a close friend that in a dream she had been commended "for her two confessions."

Speaking of herself, Mother Smaragda said, "I am a lazy monastic. My labor for my salvation is not hard. I don't have to worry about a job, I just sit in my cell and finger my prayer beads. If I had to work at saving my soul out there, sitting on a hump, in the midst of all the hustle and bustle of the world, like everyone else does, that would be another matter."

Christian faith in the world is Christian faith "out on a hump." This does not sound very nice, but it is the truth of the matter.

✦ ✦ ✦

One day Mother Smaragda told us of a woman who spent whole days at the market place selling produce from her garden. She would pull her head scarf right down on her eyes, to protect them from the bright sun, but also not to be distracted by the noise and bustle around her. All the time she recited the "Jesus prayer." There she was, praying, her eyes downcast, when suddenly an old beggar passed by, stopped and said to her: "Just say 'Lord, bless me!' and it will be easier." He said this and went on and she never saw him again. She was praying silently, of course, so he could not have heard what words she used. "This is the kind of market women and beggars we used to have!" concluded Mother Smaragda.

✦ ✦ ✦

Mother Smaragda once said, "It is impossible, I think, to explain what spiritual life is, yet it is good if you just know that it exists."

I remember a play given at the Moscow Art Theater called "At the Gates of the Kingdom." We too stand at the threshold of spiritual life, as at the gates of a kingdom.

✦ ✦ ✦

I remember Mother Smaragda's death well. It was a morning in May: I was going to church and stopped by to find out how she was. As I went up the porch steps, two nuns were struggling to bring the coffin down from the attic. It had been made ready quite a long while ago. "How is Mother?" I asked. "Poorly, very poorly ... " I went into the room where three women, probably her closest spiritual friends stood at her bed. "Read the prayers ...," one of them whispered, and I began to read. Suddenly there was another, anguished whisper: "Read, read ..." I understood that the "cup was being brought to her lips ..." Mother had used this expression when speaking of death quite a long while ago. We stood silently, not experiencing sorrow, for when a holy heart stops beating it is a sacrament, not a sorrow.

Eight or nine years later I visited the little town again and tried to find Mother's grave in the snow-covered cemetery. I barely managed to make out the top of the cross on her grave and, to the great amusement of an urchin watching me, crawled through the snowdrifts. I reached the cross like a drowning man reaches a point of safety, I cried over it, as if it were a mother's blessing.

✠ ✠ ✠

I saw Father Alexei Mechev several times, at home and when he celebrated in church. I remember the childish pleasure he took in small courtesies extended to the least "important" of his visitors, holding their overcoats for them, etc.

"Some people call me clairvoyant," he once said. "It is not clairvoyance, it's just knowing people. I can really discern what they feel, as if their feelings lay in the flat of my hand," and he turned up his thin, dry hand to illustrate his words. He was very slight of bulid, quick in his movements, with a kind of irrepressible joyousness shining from his wise, all-seeing eyes. He was so different from the usual, somewhat somber, clerical image of pre-revolutionary Moscow clergy, a real bearer of the "eternal joy" of the Easter service.

✠ ✠ ✠

Before being ordained to the priesthood my father, Father

Joseph Fudel, worked as a civil servant at the Moscow Court of Justice. He was recently married and lived with my mother in a small apartment. It happened at that time that a nun whom he knew committed a sin of adultery, was expelled from her monastery and underwent much hardship. She was young and beautiful. My mother especially remembered her beautiful long hair.

My father came home one day and told my mother that the young woman was in desperate need and homeless. "Will you mind if we take her in?" he asked. My mother burst out crying and hugged him, "In a strange feeling of gratitude ... ," she said later. The expelled nun made her home with my parents.

I believe that my father, who had never studied in a seminary, passed his final examination for the priesthood on that day. He was ordained by the remarkable Bishop Alexis of Vilno. In a letter we received after my father's death, one of his spiritual daughters wrote: "I remember his last sermon. He spoke about the Lord's Mother and seemed to be shining with joy and a sense of victory. He finished by quoting the words of Bishop Dimitri of Rostov: 'Rejoice, sinners! The righteous will be led to heaven by Saint Peter the Apostle, and the sinners by the Mother of Our Lord herself.' " This message I keep in my heart, when my heart is not dead, and on this note of joy I can end my recollections of him.

✠ ✠ ✠

The first years after the revolution, 1917–1919, were a time of amazing spiritual uplift, a kind of lightheartedness. We stood at the threshold of a new period in church history. We were terrified, watching the great black clouds gathering, and at the same time we were breathing an air of unknown spiritual freedom.

Something in the life of the Church was returning to its pristine purity and simplicity, something was coming up from underneath centuries of secularization, hypocrisy and externalism. It was the time when Rublev's icon of the Holy Trinity had its heavily bejewled silver covering of later centuries taken off. Human hearts were rediscovering the joy of the forgotten "first love." The Church was rediscovering its sacrificial character. It was a frightening and joyous time for us who were young then.

I remember many people whom I met then ... I remember N Preiss, in his gold-rimmed spectacles and a funny small cap. When he went to services in the many Moscow churches, he carried an oil-cloth satchel filled with the New Testament, the Psalter and a few books of poetry. Poetry, which he loved dearly, somehow fitted into his new way of church life. Often he performed the duties of reader during church services, and I believe he knew all the psalms by heart.

At that time several outstanding Russian intellectuals moved to Moscow and to Zagorsk. Among them was V Rosanov. Rosanov was a little old man with sharp, penetrating eyes. He seemed to isolate himself in clouds of tobacco smoke, as if seeking in them a kind of retreat from the world. He was typical of a whole generation of Russian "intelligentsia," possessing both real intelligence and an empty talkativeness, true sincerity and complete self-centeredness, a recognition of atheism as a dead-end and a wishful seeking of faith. He had a kind of half-way recognition of true faith: "Yes, there is something to it, but my own great ideas are more precious to me. Let me be..." In his memoirs, which I read recently, Berdyaev describes this kind of thinking as typical of a certain epoch. It is very persistent and barren.

I remember how, one day, N Preiss called on a friend and found Rosanov there lying on a bed, in clouds of tobacco smoke, with books piled and scattered all around him. Preiss stopped at the bed and, as if trying to penetrate a smoke screen, sternly announced, "You know, Christ really rose from the dead!"

Later, when the famine in Moscow grew worse, Preiss was homeless, starving, and infested with lice. Some friends remained hospitable, but they had to let him sleep on the floor because of the lice. One of these friends was a priest, who died in prison later in 1940. He told his wife at the end, "To die in prison is a great happiness for a priest."

Sergei Durylin had a great personal love for Jesus Christ, the kind of love that we see shine so brightly in the lives and writings of the Church Fathers and of which we were so well reminded by Dostoyevsky. Yet facts remain facts: Durylin became an Orthodox priest and then left the Church. Perhaps it would be right to say that he left the Church precisely because he became a priest, because he undertook to carry a burden too heavy for him. For anyone who is weak in spirit, though sincere and loving, it is unbearable to see Evil present at The Last Supper. To see this and to have the strength to remain a true priest, one has to have the strength to repeat continuously the apostles' question, "Is it I, Lord?" in reply to the Lord's words, "One of you will betray Me." What depth of humility, what penetration into the mystery of God's providence! Only this can save and lead each one of us in our life in the Church, especially those who serve in the sanctuary, where the Lord's Supper takes place again and again.

Such humility can be attained only by a difficult labor of faith. Durylin, at that critical time of his life, had lost his elders and remained alone (Father Anatoli of Optino and Father Alexei Mechev had both died).

✛ ✛ ✛

Bishop Tikhon (Tikhomirov) was the son of an old revolutionary leader who had organized the assasination of Czar Alexander II in 1889. For fifteen years, until his death soon after the end of the World War II, the bishop remained a recluse, living in great poverty, in a tiny room in the city of Yaroslav. Only every few years would he leave his room to vote during state elections. I remember how I once waited for a very long time in the kitchen next to his room, for him to finish his prayers. He always prayed quite alone.

When he was dying he said, "I'm going home now." Above the small table in his cell, at which he used to serve me tea, were many photos of his family and friends and his old home in Zagorsk. Huge crowds attended his funeral and the service was celebrated by the local bishop, specifically at the request of the Patriarch. "Is it not strange," he said in his sermon, "we've lived here so long and we never knew we had a great light hidden among us."

I am sure many people wonder, "Why? What's the use of seclusion, of eremitic life?" Love for people does not exclude the need for the desert. Perhaps each one of us needs a little bit of desert to strengthen his capacity to love. A Russian poet said, "the desert listens to God and stars talk to each other."

✛ ✛ ✛

An old peasant woman lay dying. She kept on asking her

daughter to go fetch a priest so that she could receive Holy Communion. But it was a long trip to the only church that was still open and, in the bitter winter weather, the daughter kept putting it off. One night the dying woman asked her six-year old granddaughter for a drink. When a cup of water was given to her, the people in the room thought they heard the words of the communion hymn, "Receive the Body of Christ."

Father Seraphim (Batiugov) used to say, "If there is no possibility for you to receive Holy Communion and yet you feel an inexorable need for it, then just read all the 'Prayers in Preparation for Holy Communion' and give yourself up to God's will and providence."

✤ ✤ ✤

In 1923 many bishops were exiled at the same time to Zyrian. One of them was accompanied voluntarily by the bishop's spiritual son, a young layman. We were all impressed by the boy; he had taken a vow of silence and never said a word. When necessary, he used sign language. Only recently had he graduated from high school. I remember his eyes, they were kindly and cheerful. He went barefoot and wore a long shirt without a belt. It happened once that he slept over at my place. When night came, I thought he'd pray for a very long time. I half expected him to wear a heavy cross and chains, like the innocent Grisha Tolstoy described in his *Childhood and Boyhood*. But all he did was ask me for something by sign, then he crossed himself and settled down for the night. The next day he surprised me again; I had some books about the lives of saints and put them purposely on a table in the room where he was to sleep. "That will be a treat for him!" I thought rather foolishly. He opened a book, began reading, then laid it aside and did not touch it again.

We speak, write, think, read about spirituality and spiritual feats, but saints are silent and their effort is silent.

✠ ✠ ✠

They began building the Moscow subway in the thirties. A priest, Father Michael Schlick, said to me in 1936, "Pray everywhere. What a joy it will be to feel, riding on the subway, that heaven is open and there are no bars to prayer." Obviously the Moscow subway was already hallowed by Father Michael's prayer. He perished in 1938.

I remember his saying, when speaking about prayer, that not only the "Jesus Prayer" could be used constantly. He quoted Saint Paul's words, "pray at all times in the spirit with all prayers ..." Bishop Theophan the Recluse says the same thing.

In a prison camp, a Valamo monk, Father Spiridon, taught those of us who felt a special need for the prayers of Mary the Theotokos to say, "Jesus Christ, Son of God, through the prayers of the Theotokos, have mercy on us." On us who are not lost.

✠ ✠ ✠

From 1948 until 1951 I lived in a village in Siberia where there were many peasants exiled from Lithuania, most of them Roman Catholic. On Sundays, their young women and girls would attend the service at our Orthodox Church, bringing their Catholic prayer books, reverently kneeling down and praying. A few men came too. No arguments on doctrinal differences ever arose between us, no one attempted to measure the depth of either side's error. Without any "ecumenical" preparation, a union of the Church was being realized. Probably some day such a reunion on a universal scale will take place in this very way, not at ecumenical conferences, but in a thunderstorm of historical events, in prayer, and in the clear realization that there is only one haven for all, the Holy Spirit.

I remember how we feared to break the peaceful quiet of this unexpected joy. We firmly kept at arm's length the naive curiosity of our village lads pressing in on the kneeling figures of the women with their unfamiliar beads in their hands.

Yet, at the same little wooden church I was once very much upset. It was Great Lent and confessions were being heard in church. I came outside and sat down on a bench where two young women were already resting. We began to talk. They had walked all the way from a village some 35-40 kilometers away. They lived together, one was a Catholic, the other Orthodox, and our Orthodox church was the closest to their village. Suddenly, I noticed that the Orthodox young woman had tears in her eyes. I learned that she had brought only three roubles and Father had told the man in charge of the candle sales that five roubles should be paid for confession (that was at the old rouble rate). The woman did not judge the priest, she did not want to convert to Catholicism, she just wept. I saw these tears and I think that all of us must see them.

After my return to Moscow from exile in 1925, I came to the church where Father Valentin Sventitsky was serving liturgy. I came rather late. When I saw his face as he read the final prayer (the "prayer before the ambo"), I was struck by his expression. It was a real shock to watch the face of a man who had just made a sacrifice of himself, in the most real and painful sense of the word. He came out to us, without noticing us, shaken by his experience. At that moment I understood the meaning of the stigmata.

Right there I gave proof of my ignorance. Instead of waiting until later, I entered the sanctuary and began speaking about the matter that was on my mind. He raised his hand to stop me, "Only those who believe in God can enter here," he said. "Do you believe?" We had not seen each other for three years, he had heard things about me that were not true, and he wanted to make sure that he could admit me to his "holy of holies."

Later during my endless wanderings through the corridors of the Butyrka prison in Moscow, I suddenly met Father Valentin Sventitsky. Rather foolishly I asked him, "Where are you going?" His fact lit up with a kind of inner warmth as he answered, "To be with you!" He was always such a reserved man, severe, exclusive, but that day I felt a ray of kindly, all-seeing saintliness shining at me. He approached my soul, which was in need of his help. He was like a "starets." This is what prison life can make you see. Later I read many of Father Valentin's sermons and never did I find in them a single ray of the light I saw that day in Butyrka prison.

Not far from the town of Voronezh, at the very edge of a great state forest, lived an old woman with her unmarried daughter Sasha. Sasha was crippled by a childhood accident, which left her quite deaf. Their hut stood somewhat aside from the village, the forest just behind it, and a large meadow in front. There was always a strange stillness about the house, no noise, no talking, and a great peacefulness. Swallows that nested in the eaves of the roof flew into the room quite regularly. They hunted for bugs and flies and then settled on the frame of a large mirror and looked into it with interest.

In the daytime Sasha took their cow to graze in the forest. There were plenty of wild animals there, and also men who might harm her. Every time she went into the woods, she would say, "Now, Lord, You look out for me!" And He did.

I have not seen them for more than twenty years. The old mother died and I don't know what happened to Sasha. I share their faith, and when I am at peace, I share their stillness. I hope that in the Kingdom of Heaven I will be allowed to enter their house with the friendly swallows.

✣ ✣ ✣

A woman was dying in a hospital ward and her end would not come. She had no friends, no relatives, no one. At last, one night, she called the nurse's aide on duty, a woman who had shown her compassion. She asked her to receive her confession, a terrible confession for all her life. It was impossible to have a priest come. The nurse accepted the confession and the next morning took it to church. The sick woman died that same evening.

✣ ✣ ✣

I know some young men who became believers in their twenties. If their parents are militant atheists, these young Christians "invent" ill health, pretend to have ulcers, in order to be able to keep fasts at home. They really enter a desert more lonely than the ancient desert of Egypt. In those deserts of antiquity a hermit could become exhausted, but he could think of every human soul as a source of living water, an oasis. In the desert of a great modern city, almost every human being seems to be a desert in himself.

Lord, help us! Lord, help us! Your people, O Lord, are crying to you.

Tania, a young art specialist, began collecting icons. She was questioned: "Are you a believer?" She denied it: "I do not believe." Later she had a nervous breakdown and received an insulin shock treatment. Lying unconscious, she kept asking loudly: "Do you exist, O God? Tell me, do You exist?"

I met Paul "the fool in Christ" in 1947 in Minusinsk. He was very dear to my heart and I believe him to be a true saint. He did not actually behave as a fool, he simply went his way among people without noticing their demands nor conforming to the general expectation that each person must be like everyone else. He did not notice this because he was absorbed in some deep concern of his own, which only he understood. Sometimes, when he walked down a street and someone gave him alms, he would stop and remain for a long time absorbed in prayer for the person who had given him help, or perhaps for those who had not helped him?

Quite unexpectedly Paul would turn up in our town — perhaps released from some labor camp — all ragged, tattered and torn, not an old man really, but haggard, exhausted by something he had gone through. His exhaustion was obvious, but he was never gloomy. Theophan the Recluse wrote to his spiritual children: "Never be gloomy, never sulk."

One day I saw Paul sitting on the ground near the church, and I put some apples in his lap. He raised his eyes and said lovingly: "Thank you, brother." Later I met him in the market place and asked him to pray for me. The last time I saw him was on Good Friday, when we all stood with lighted candles in church, surrounding the icon of Jesus Christ in the tomb (*epitaphion*). We, truly, were seeing off our Saviour to His earthly death. Paul stood in the crowd, a little ahead of me, with no candle in his hands. I passed on to him my own. He turned back and without raising his eyes, blessed me with the candle.

Thirty years have passed since then, yet I still feel the warmth of the candle reaching from him to me.

✣ ✣ ✣

During the war a priest, Father Vladimir Krivolutsky, stayed with us for some time. All day long he was busy with people; he argued, he brought people together, he rejoiced with us, he shared our fears. At night, when he retired, and only then, would he take his prayer beads, settle down in bed with the blanket drawn over his head, and retire to his inner "desert."

Eternity is more visible in the desert. Bishop Ignatius Brianchaninov used to say that we must learn to look at eternity before we enter its immeasurable space.

✣ ✣ ✣

In 1959 two women made a trip to visit Mother Matriosha. People called her "Mother" although she was not a nun. She lived in proximity of the famous "Kulikovo Pole," in a small hut at the walls of a former monastery, now closed. By that time "Mother Matriosha" was quite old, over eighty. She had never been married, and in her youth had lived with her mother in extreme poverty. Her work was to read the psalter over the bodies of the deceased, according to the ancient Russian custom. At one time, when Matriosha was still young, there was a bad epidemic of cholera, and people died in great numbers. She would spend nights in the homes of the bereaved and come home exhausted. At home her mother would present her with further requests: "Matriosha, they sent for you. They are very poor and cannot pay anyone else. You really must go." Matriosha would say that she was too tired, but her mother insisted: "Go, Matriosha, what can they do? They are so poor!" And Matriosha would heave a sigh of fatigue and start off again and spend night after night reading prayers and psalms, often in unheated, drafty rooms.

By the time I knew her she lived in an old sunken hut, where she lay on a kind of wooden shelf that served her as a cot. The only heat was provided by candles which she lit to read offices and to pray. Candles were the one gift she accepted from her visitors, but she greeted everyone loving-ly, even if she occasionally scolded some people. To those who knew no prayers, she gave manuscript copies made by some of her literate disciples. Her niece brought her food, but Matriosha refused to move into a more comfortable and warm home and remained in her hut until the end, in constant prayer for people.

✠ ✠ ✠

Sometimes, when I watch older and younger people traveling on the subway, the younger seem purer.

Father Alexander Elchaninov wonders whether the words of Saint Paul, "All who have sinned without the law, will also perish," are not to be understood in the sense that those who "have no law," but did not sin, will be saved?

Now that the new paganism is so well established in all the world, there are many young people who know nothing about Christianity. Don't the words of Saint Paul, "The law is written in their hearts," apply to them?

Father Nectary of Optino said, "A pious Hindu who believes in God and, to the best of his ability, carries out His will, will surely be saved." And then he added, "But one who knows Christianity, yet seeks mystical Hindu experiences, turns away from salvation."

Father Nectary, the Optino elder, was greatly interested in the futuristic poet Khlebnikov and said about Alexander Blok after his death, "He is in heaven. Tell his mother not to worry, she can be sure of this."

✣ ✣ ✣

"I have no daring because of my sins" (Prayer of the sixth hour); yet Father Golubtsov had daring in his hour of death. He said to his brother, "Sing me my favorite prokeimenon," and his brother chanted: "Blessed before God is the demise of His holy ones."

On the 40th day after Father Golubtsov's death, when the flowers on his grave were still not quite dry, we gathered there again, some of us strangers to each other, others close friends. The weather was not too harsh. We stood, crowded in the narrow passages between the graves. No religious service could be performed, but suddenly we heard someone reciting the memorial prayers, in a low voice, unhesitatingly, with the assurance of great familiarity. It was a man we did not know, dressed in civilian clothes, clean shaven, elderly, though not really old. Suddenly we all felt closer to each other, closer to heaven. When the man finished, he bowed deeply at the grave and moved away. We whispered as he passed us by, "Thank you, thank you!"

✣ ✣ ✣

God Himself searches out His disciples. Both Pascal and Florensky say that when God approaches an individual, He comes not as the God of philosophers and scientists, but as the God of Abraham, Isaac and Jacob, leading man by the hand.

The painting by Ivanov, Christ's apparition to the people, is well known to us. Christ appears to the soul of each person called to God within the measure of the individual's capacities. A human heart may be startled by some small occurence, a Gospel book found among trash thrown out by a neighbor, a strange dream, a beautiful icon, sometimes an encounter with a saintly and loving person. Saint Symeon the New Theologian said, "If Christ does not manifest Himself to us, we can neither believe in Him, nor love Him truly."

I was recently told the story of a young, unbelieving Jewish girl. In a dream she saw herself running away, in deathly terror, from some horrible danger. Suddenly, she saw a Crucifix and threw herself at it, with a sense of finding safety in it. When she woke up, she began looking for the church of the Crucified.

Christ's apparition is the birth of His image within an individual soul, it is a personal experience of the words *Ecco Homo*. We can believe only when we have begun to love. Saint Symeon says, "One who cannot love God, cannot believe in Him."

Out of every one hundred people standing in church, at best there may be no more than two or three men or three women younger than fifty. Earlier, in the twenties, we used to say, "The Church is left to the women!," and we thought of the myrrh-bearing women. In those earlier days there were many girls and young women attending church services. Now we have to say "The Church is left to the old women!" And we are lucky if they are not ill-tempered. Some of the young Christians who are lucky enough to live in Moscow have become part of a small group of faithful young believers. They are inclined to think that "everything is in order," and they are not conscious of the terrible process of de-christianization going on in Russia. They do not realize that many millions of people live completely outside the Church, and the churches remain empty. Cities and villages compete for a faster pace in abandoning all Christian faith, and it seems the villages are winning. Following some sort of orderly process Christianity returns to its earliest forms, not only spiritually, but geographically as well. It moves from villages to large cities: the "Rome," "Ephesus," "Antioch" and "Corinth" of our day. These will be the new Christian communities of the last times, surrounded by millions of unbelievers and awaiting to discover new prophets and old apostles.

✤ ✤ ✤

In one of the central regions of Russia, so often described by Turgenev, there lived in the nineteen forties a pilgrim called Ilarion. He was of Jewish origin, a tailor by profession. We did not know how he had become a Christian or acquired the spiritual authority that he had. Perhaps he was a disciple of some Optino monk, many of whom were scattered in towns and villages after the closing of the monastery.

I had never met him, but I knew a number of people who, even years after his death, lived in the atmosphere of his spiritual heritage. Of course, he will never be mentioned in any church report or in church history. He fulfilled his apostolic mission and left us. Yet even today there are always fresh flowers on his grave in the church yard, and candles are lit there on holy days. A woman I knew, Katia, told me that he had once asked her to stay for the night in her house. "I woke up at night and heard him singing softly in his corner, near the stove, 'We who mystically represent the cherubim ...' "

Thus do the righteous spend their nights, and the surrounding darkness does not frighten them.

Towards the end of World War II, a small band of six or eight soldiers broke out of an enemy encirclement and were trying to find their way home. They followed the roads to the East, or went straight through forests and fields to avoid being recaptured by the Germans. One evening, quite exhausted, knee-deep in snow, they found themselves at the edge of a field. "I guess that's the end for us ... ," one of them said. Suddenly they saw light not far away and went towards it. They found a tiny hut, standing all by itself, on a hillock in the middle of the field. One of them knocked, entered and found an old man sitting there, mending felt shoes. The soldier did not have to beg for hospitality; the old man invited them to come in and stay the night. The hut was warm, they all tumbled down on the floor and, exhausted, fell asleep right away. When they woke up it was daylight. They were huddled together, not on the floor of a hut, but on the ground, lightly covered with snow. There was no roof above them, just open sky. In the early morning stillness they could hear a distant church bell ringing. All this took place in Western Ukraine. The soldiers jumped up and, guided by the bell, found the church. As they entered it, one of them saw an icon of Saint Nicholas and said: "This was our host!"

At the beginning of the Germans' advance in World War II, their troops almost reached Zagorsk. A woman living in that city was returning home from her late-night shift in a local factory. It was the feast of Saint Sergius. The sun was rising, the grass and flowers were glistening in the early light. Yet, neither the sunrise nor the flowers drew her attention for she was too full of fear at the approach of the fighting. Her small children were living with her in her home.

Suddenly she met a woman she did not know, and they continued on their way together. The stranger said, "Don't be afraid. We are under the protection of Saint Sergius. He said that his city would remain whole. You might believe this better if I tell you that an elder, Father Alexei, lived here in the twenties. He died here, too. When the authorities began to open up graves and desecrate the relics, Father Alexei was greatly distressed and he prayed continuously, wondering why God allowed such things. Then, one evening, as he stood at prayer, he saw Saint Sergius standing at prayer next to him. The Saint said, "Pray and fast for three days and I will tell you what you need to know." For two more nights Saint Sergius joined Father Alexei at prayer, and Father Alexei fasted, eating only holy bread. On the third day the Saint said, "When living people have to go through great suffering, it is necessary that the bodies of those who died share this suffering with them. I offered up my body, so that my city might remain whole."

"We thought at the time," added the strange woman, "that these words referred to the typhus epidemic of those days, but now we understand what he had in mind."

The woman listened to the story, and when she reached home — where everyone was still sound asleep — she sat down on the porch steps. Strangely at peace, she noticed for the first time the grass, the flowers, the bright sunshine.

Saint Sergius of Radonezh lived in the fourteenth century. Father Alexei Zasimovsky was a saint living in the twentieth century. There are always saints in the life of the Church.

Recently I was told a story about three little boys, Boria, Misha and Serezha, 10 and 11 years old, who lived in Zagorsk during the German advance on Moscow. On August 27th, on the eve of the Dormition, they went into the forest to collect firewood. As it began to grow dark, the boys realized they had lost their way. For a long time they tried to get their bearings, and at last one of them said, "I think we should try to pray ..." They decided Misha had to do this "Because you, Misha, know how to ..." Misha made the sign of the cross several times and they again began looking for the road, but it was no use. Suddenly they saw a twinkling light far away, behind the trees. "It must be a forester's hut!" they thought, and they went towards the light. They came to a little meadow and saw an old man. He had "a hat, like a priest," and held a big cross in his right hand and in his left hand there was something "that he was waving about" (a censer?). The boys were scared, they nudged Misha to step forward, "Pray, pray, Misha, you know how ..." Misha began to pray and "the old man in the priest's hat" blessed them with the cross. Then suddenly, they realized he was pointing with his cross to a path, the path they were looking for, and they ran following it. When they got out of the woods and were back again in familiar surroundings, they realized that they had been following not a real path, but a ray of light.

Right there they decided that early the next morning they would go to church. Grown-ups whom they told about their adventure realized that it must have been Saint Sergius blessing the city. The Germans did not reach Zagorsk.

Friends used to call Father Dimitri Kruchkov "the Gardener." During the thirties he was obliged to give up his priestly functions and for several years was employed as gardener in some prestigious institution. At the same time, he remained a disciple and spiritual son of Father Seraphim (Batiugov), and his gardening profession did not save him from being arrested and sent to Siberia in 1946. This is when I met him. He was not an intellectual or academically minded. He was rather worldly in a way, liked to have a drink of vodka, and smoked a lot. But he was a man of straightforward and honest faith. I remember one of the stories he told me. While he was still an active priest, he suffered from excruciating headaches which almost made him lose consciousness. One day he felt a headache beginning during a solemn service in a large Moscow cathedral. It was an All-Night Vigil service, on the eve of the feast of Saint Seraphim, at which a number of priests took part. They stood in two rows, facing the icon of the saint. "Suddenly," said Father Dimitri, "I felt that I could not bear the pain any more. I left my place, went up to the icon and, with everyone watching me, dipped my finger in one of the oil-burning vigil lights and made a sign of the cross on my forehead. The pain stopped at the very same instant and I returned to my place. I never suffered from headaches again."

It is not the miraculous aspect of the incident that impressed me, but the way it was linked to simple, straightforward faith, unembarrassed, unafraid to disrupt the ceremonial order and ritual. Only a willingness to confess one's faith, even in such ways as Father Dimitri's, can save us and our world.

In this same Siberian prison there was another priest, Father Ivan "the Carpenter," as well as Father Dimitri "the

Gardener." He lived in the town of Kasimov, working as a carpenter because he belonged to the church group called "non-commemorators," who refused to pray for the government or for Metropolitan Sergius. They say that when Saint John Chrysostom was exiled and practically condemned to a slow death, some of his disciples also formed a splinter group within the Church. It existed for some thirty years, until the relics of the saint were solemnly brought back to Constantinople.

Father Ivan had an old, very Russian face, quite icon-like. He was mild and quiet, but in the matter of offering prayers for authorities he was firm and insistent. "He is a fanatic!" Father Dimitri "the Gardener" used to say crossly. I remember so well the two of them, walking together, both of them bearded and with no clothes on — they were in line to the prison bathhouse — waiting for those few blessed minutes of warmth and almost-hot water, while arguing about "commemorating" and "not commemorating" civil authorities during church services.

I remember also the prison cell, so crowded we could scarcely breathe, and the "cell choir" performing a folk song for my personal benefit. I remember celebrating Christmas with a Lutheran co-prisoner, for the first time in my life according to the new calendar.

During my imprisonment there were so many people, endless rows of people who went swiftly by, but somehow our hearts were yearning to keep in touch, to find each other again in the safer harbor of Christ. I am no theologian. I do not know what this longing is. Maybe it is not necessary to know — one just has to follow it.

The convoy from Moscow to Novosibirsk was a difficult one. Somewhere on the way we stopped, were lined up, and marched to the transit prison building. There were no police dogs. Father John "the Carpenter" and I were the last ones in line, and behind us walked the guard, a good-natured young soldier, armed with a gun. Father John fell down. He had not stumbled, he just had no strength to go on, and he lay there, white-faced. Somehow we managed to prop him up. The soldier was obviously worried about the delay, but he also felt compassion. "Get up, Father, get up!" Later, on Old-Calendar Christmas night, we were lying next to each other in the barracks in Novosibirsk. Gradually everything quieted down, a storyteller finished his adventure crime story, and people began to snore. Then, very quietly, without raising his voice, Father John began to sing: "Christ is born. Glorify Him, Christ comes from heaven, meet ye Him ..." Then he murmured, "I've forgotten the 8th irmos. My head is no good ... Getting weaker and weaker ... maybe you, Sergei, remember?" I was so sorry, but I also could not remember the verse. It goes: "The furnace moist with dew was the image and figure of a wonder past nature ..."

Two days later we were separated. I continued on my way to Krasnoyarsk together with Father Dimitri "the Gardener" — the one "who commemorated the authorities."

The elder Father Seraphim (Batiugov) stayed for twelve years in seclusion in his cell, not in a monastery but in a private home in Zagorsk. He remained there until his death in 1942. His decision to retire in this way was an act of obedience to the blessed Maria Ivanovna of the Diveyevo Convent. During a visit with her, he spoke with enthusiasm of his work in a Moscow parish. She interrupted him, saying, "You must become a recluse." Father Seraphim argued, giving good reasons against such a decision, but again she told him to relinquish the world. Then Father Seraphim said, "Bless me, Mother." He retired into seculsion and remained a hermit until the end of his life. A simple woman, endowed with no priestly authority, changed the course of life of a highly placed priest simply on the strength of her personal holiness.

Normal relationships that we see on the surface of church life are quite different when a greater depth is reached. I remember seeing bishops make prostrations before a simple monk who was their spiritual father.

Holy people have their own rules. I was told by Father Seraphim that, when he was rector in a parish church, a bishop was serving there regularly. A matter of spiritual importance arose in which the priest and the bishop disagreed. Father Seraphim was greatly concerned about the situation. Finally Father Nectary of Optino Monastery confirmed Father Seraphim's opinion, and he then acted as rector of the parish, against the opinion of a bishop. The matter was decided according to the judgement of a simple Optino monk. This would have been impossible in the hierarchal structure of the church in Rome.

I remember Father Seraphim so vividly, his silver, shoulder-length hair and his informal, unclerical dress. He wore a "Tolstoy" style tunic, and no cassock. Perhaps he is testing me. "You are so indulgent," he says, "you pay no attention to the way I dress." "Father!" I exclaim quite sincerely, "What do clothes matter?" He does not answer me, but he looks pleased. He feels there are no barriers between me and his warm concern for my life, no external difficulties in our communication with each other.

The warmth of a saintly soul thaws the ice in our hearts. In some ways, I find it difficult to be with an "elder," but at the same time I feel as if I were again an infant in my mother's womb. Perhaps unborn infants do not always feel comfortable in their mother's womb. I think the influence of an "elder" on his spiritual son or daughter can be defined thus: endless human concern for each one who comes to him, or needs his help, combined with a superhuman, supernatural power and vision.

I remember copying a letter at Father Seraphim's request, addressed to his spiritual daughter. It began with the words: "My beloved child ..."

I remember his standing with us at prayer in his belted cassock, in a short monastic "half-mantle." As we pray, he occasionally blesses someone, making the sign of the cross in space, in the direction of an absent spiritual child. Sometimes he stops the reader and begins to read the prayer himself, then stops suddenly, sighing heavily. We remain silent too and wait, for we know that at this very moment his prayer has not stopped, but that he is crying unto God. Sometimes he would start reading prayers in the regular formal monotone, but suddenly his voice would break, become tense, his eyes filled with tears. This might last several minutes, interrupting the regular monastic type of prayer. It could be "uncomfortable" to pray with him, just as it is "uncomfortable" for a beginner to follow an experienced swimmer into deep water.

One day Father Vladimir Krivolutsky mentioned to Father Seraphim his concern and criticism of such a manner of prayer. Father Seraphim listened silently but did not change.

I suppose we would have felt even more "uncomfortable" at a worship gathering of the Apostles, when simple laymen received revelations, spoke in tongues, prophesied ... For us this kind of worship is a subject for historic research. For saintly people it is a reality. Father Seraphim had great respect for church rubrics and believed that any careless or arrogant breaking of church regulations is disastrous (he once told me, "outside church rubric the devil's claws are waiting to snatch us"). Yet, when he served, he actually seemed to enter into a form of church life which in many ways resembled that of the early Christian Church.

During the years when Father Seraphim Batiugov visited us, we had a simple woman living with our family. She was a former nun, who had left her home at a very early age to enter a monastery, but at the time I remember her she wore ordinary clothes and paid no special attention to rules of fasting. Her heart was full of compassion for all people. Father Seraphim used to say that she moved through life with angelic steps. She died at our home on the morning of Easter Eve, conscious until the very last moment, fully assured that she was not being destroyed by death, just entering a new life.

She was quite temperamental and heartily disliked poorly celebrated church services. This really upset Father Seraphim, especially when he saw her going off to work in the kitchen garden just as he would be putting on his *epitrachelion* to begin a service in our home. He would go on reading and chanting, but from time to time he threw anguished glances at the figure bent over weeding in the kitchen garden. One day, as he was leaving us again for a longer time and was saying goodby to us, he suddenly bowed down in a prostration before this simple woman.

Another memory of Father Seraphim comes to my mind. One early winter morning I heard someone knocking at the door. "Who's there?" I called, and heard the gentle monastic greeting, "Jesus Christ, Son of God, have mercy on us!" I did not expect Father Seraphim and was so overjoyed to see him, that instead of giving the expected reply, "Amen," I called out "Father, it's you! How wonderful!" As I opened the door, I saw his face, so joyful and pleased because he, the wanderer, was expected and beloved.

Father Seraphim said grace before meals. He also prayed at the end of meals, usually reciting several prayers, reading them with special love, as if he were encouraging us to follow him along a path leading from ordinary food to new unfathomable horizons. These "after meal" prayers usually started with his favorite short one, "The poor will eat and their hunger will be filled and those who seek God will glorify Him. Their hearts will be alive forever."

This reminds me of the wise saying of Silouan of Mount Athos about how much we should eat: "We must eat as much as is necessary to make us want to pray after partaking of food." This means that if food does not interrupt our prayerful constancy, it is not overabundant.

I came to take leave of Father Seraphim on February 19, 1942, a few hours before he died. He had already warned those nearest to him of his approaching death. He was lying down, his face covered with some light veil, perhaps symbolic of the seclusion he had so ardently wished for. During his lifetime he had never been able to become a real recluse, because he was always surrounded by his spiritual children. Maybe we should not have been looking at his face, as it was gradually being enlightened?

One of the women taking care of him said: "Father, Sergei Iosifovich has come to take leave." Then I heard his usual gentle greeting, as if it were coming from the depths of some other world, "Holy Theotokos, save us!" He said it a second time, a little louder. This was the prayer with which he always greeted his spiritual children (using for the verb "save," the specific Russian form which means a repeated action, as if he wanted to express our continuous, repeated need for salvation). Then there was a long silence.

I saw that his attendants had already prepared a container with a spadeful of earth brought from Diveyevo (the Monastery founded by Saint Seraphim of Sarov, which is now closed). This earth, trodden by the feet of the saint, was to be placed in the bier, also prepared a long time ago.

When he was told that I was leaving, I again heard his almost inaudible yet tense whisper, "Go with God. God bless you all!"

I wish I had the spiritual power to pass on his blessing to all those who had perhaps never met a saint. We, the old ones, and surely "the fearful and unfaithful ones," probably are still there, not yet completely deprived of reason and heart, to pass on our only treasure — the blessing of the saints. These are the saints through whom we saw a glimpse of the heavenly eternity of the Church of the Lamb. Knowledge of this treasure shapes our old days. Even the horror of seeing the "Church's double" does not make us condemn those who, in one way or another, accept this double and become part of it. They have probably never known saintly people, such as we have known; they have never had the living experience of the Holy Church. They have never been gently embraced by an elder, never heard the words, "My beloved child …," fiery words which burn away our unbelief and even our sins.

The holy heart of such saints is truly the House of God, Who comes and abides in them, according to the words of the Gospel. This is the Church and we can stand at its walls.

✠ ✠ ✠

Always, and especially now, religious truth has power only when it is expressed in words proved and supported by the life of the one who says them. If you cannot prove, don't speak. The world needs saints, not philosophers or speakers. "The Kingdom of God does not consist in talk, but in power," we are told (1 Co 4:20).

I was twenty years old when I went to see Father Nectary of the Optino Monastery. There was no one else in his reception room and I waited for a short while, surprised by the unusual quiet and silence. The Elder, whom I saw for the first time, came in quickly. He gave me his blessing and right away, without any introductory words, without waiting for me to say anything, asked "Are you engaged to be married?" Without waiting for my answer, he continued, "Go to his Beatitude Patriarch Tikhon and beg him to ordain you. The path of priesthood is opening up for you."

I kept silent, stunned, for I had expected nothing of the kind.

"Don't be afraid," he said. "Follow your path and God will help you in everything. If you refuse now, you will suffer much in your life."

He stood up, gave me his blessing and left. This was the first call that I heard and I did not respond to it.

The second call was even clearer. It came in 1939 and was given by another elder, Father Seraphim (Batiugov) (the one who robed Father Nectary of Optino for the "great Schema"). Father Seraphim did not speak of the priesthood, but about faith and living according to faith. This time, with Father Seraphim, I did not feel embarrassed. I felt strong and sure and even wrote a poem which Father Seraphim liked so well that he copied it and showed it to some others.

Still, I did not respond to the call. My poem remained a poem and I did not begin my service. The words of Father Nectary about the suffering that was waiting for me came true. Now I want to ask everyone to forgive me; I want to make obeisance to all. Whoever has received knowledge of light and darkness, and did not choose light, bears a heavy burden of guilt.

✣ ✣ ✣

Dostoyevsky said somewhere, "Each one of us could have shone with the light of the Only Sinless One, but did not shine."

It is quite clear to me that, in a sense, I am dying without having borne fruit. This is not self-disparagement, it is an evaluation of my character.

More than this, somehow such an evaluation is part of my hope for forgiveness and of my gratitude for my life.

✣ ✣ ✣

Yes, there are times when boundless gratitude fills one's heart — gratitude for life, for this earth, which is "God's footstool," for every smile you encounter in passing.

Sometimes, walking down the street or leaving a store, you whisper, as after receiving Holy Communion: "Glory to Thee, O God, Glory to Thee!"

We have seen a lot of evil in the world, and within the church enclosure too, and most of all within ourselves. But somehow our heart is filled only with gratitude, with hope. Probably because God "bears all things, believes all things endures all things" (1 Co 13:7); and, perhaps, He accepts our yearning for righteousness as if it were righteousness itself. Great is His mercy! Macarius the Great said: "A human soul becomes part of the Church not because of what it has done, but because it experienced the desire for it."

O Lord, let it be so!

GLOSSARY

AMBO: Slightly elevated platform in front of the sanctuary inside the church.

AMVROSY, Elder of Optino Monastery, 1812–1891: Well-known spiritual advisor and guide, called "elder." He influenced many of the elite of Russian intelligentsia. Was visited by Tolstoy, Dostoyevsky, Solovyev and many others.

ANTIPHONS: Liturgical hymns that used to be sung "antiphonally," alternatively by two choirs.

ANTHONY, Metropolitan Anthony Bloom, 1914– : Head of the Russian Orthodox Church in England under the jurisdiction of the Moscow patriarchate. His family left Russia after the Revolution of 1917 and settled in France, where he studied and received his doctorate in medicine. Served as an officer in the French Army during World War II. In 1947 took monastic vows privately, was ordained in 1949, consecrated Bishop in 1958. Well-known for his sermons and writings.

ARBAT: Name of well-known old street in Moscow.

AFANASI (Sakharov), Bishop, 1887–1962: Leader of the so-called "catacomb church" in the USSR which did not recognize Patriarch Sergius as head of the Russian Orthodox Church. He was reconciled with Sergius' successor, Patriarch Alexei.

AKATHISTOS: A sequence of prayers of praise—twelve "kontakions" and twelve "ikos" addressed to Jesus Christ, His Mother, or saints. Very popular in Russia.

BATIUGOV (BATUKOV), Father Seraphim, 1880–1942: Educated professionally as an engineer, he came under the influence of the Optino Monastery "elders," studied theology and was ordained priest in 1919. Took monastic vows in 1922. Was strongly opposed to Patriarch Sergius' declaration of loyalty to the Soviet Government and left his parish, living secretly in friends' homes. He finally settled in a small private house in Zagorsk where he celebrated services clandestinely. Many sought his advice and guidance.

BLOK, Alexander, 1880–1921: Russian poet. Recognized leader of the "symbolist" movement.

BRIANCHANINOV, Bishop Ignatius, 1807–1867: Was born to an upper-class Russian family and had difficulty in obtaining permission to become a monk at the age of 20. Was ordained bishop in 1857 but retired because of ill health. His religious books and letters were widely read in Russia.

BULGAKOV, Father Sergius, 1871–1944: Economist, philosopher, theologian, priest; a remarkable Russian intellectual who switched from Marxism to Orthodox Christian faith. Was ordained priest in 1918. Was exiled from Russia after the revolution of 1917 and settled in France. Was dean of the Saint Sergius Theological Institute in Paris, France.

DURYLIN, Sergei, 1871–1959: A brilliant Russian intellectual, deeply influenced by his contacts with Optino Monastery. Was ordained a priest in 1918, but left the priesthood in 1927.

DVADTSATKA: "Twenty," a group of twenty. According to law concerning parish organization in USSR, all administrative power belongs to a group of twenty persons, or, rather, to its executive committee of three. The local authorities exert strong influence on the election of the executive committee.

ELCHANINOV, Father Alexander, 1881–1934: Close friend of Father Paul Florensky since their school days in Tiflis, Russia. Outstanding teacher and educator. Emigrated from Russia in 1920 and settled in France. Under the influence of Father Sergius Bulgakov became priest. Died eight years later. His widow published a collection of his writings under the title *The Diary of a Russian Priest*.

FLORENSKY, Father Paul, 1882–1943?: One of the major figures of the theological and cultural rebirth in Russia in the first decades of the 20th century. His major work, however, *The Pillar and Foundation of Truth*, has remained controversial. He was also a brilliant mathematician and scientist, and when the Theological Seminary was closed in 1919, he turned to scientific work. He was arrested in 1933, sentenced to ten years of hard labor and from 1937 deprived of the right to correspond with his family. Official date of his death: December 15, 1943, place unknown.

GOLUBTSOV, Father Nicholas, 1900–1962: Graduated from an Agricultural College in 1920 and for twenty-five years worked in this field. Was ordained priest in 1949 and became a humble, kindly, tireless parish priest in Moscow.

ICON OF OUR LADY OF VLADIMIR: a remarkable icon, painted probably in the XIIth century, brought from Byzantium to Kiev, then taken to Vladimir and finally to Moscow. Now exhibited in the Tretiakov Art Gallery in Moscow. According to ancient tradition the likeness was painted by the Evangelist Luke.

IKOS: see *AKATHISTOS*

ILLARION (Troitsky), Bishop, 1886–1929: Professor at the Theological Seminary in Zagorsk. Was arrested in 1920 and then in 1923. Author of the famous letter from the churchmen imprisoned in the Solovetski Labor Camp to the Soviet government which proclaimed principles of separation between Church and State, as opposed to the subservience to the state proclaimed by Patriarch Sergius. Died in a Leningrad prison.

IRMOS: The first verse of each of the nine canticles making up a "canon" — a set of readings and hymns.

JOHN, Father John of Kronstadt, 1829–1908: Parish priest in the port town of Kronstadt in the vicinity of Petersburg who devoted himself to the service of the destitute and alcoholics there. He became widely known for the intensity of his prayer and many cases of healing and help in answer to his prayers.

KHLEBNIKOV, Vladimir, 1885–1922: A Russian Futurist poet.

KHOMYAKOV, A S, 1804–1860: Founder of the Slavophile movement. Poet and lay theologian.

KONTAKION: see *AKATHISTOS*

KRIVOCHEINE, Bishop Vasili, 1900–1985: Son of a states-
man in imperial Russia, a volunteer in the White Army during
the Civil War of 1918–1919, he became part of the Russian
emigre community in France, studied at the Sorbonne and St
Sergius Institute in Paris. In 1924 became a monk at Mount
Athos, but was forced to leave in 1950. Was ordained priest and
bishop in England, under the jurisdiction of the Moscow
Patriarchate. Attended the Moscow Church Council in 1917.
Died in 1985 during a visit to Russia.

KULIKOVO POLE: Battlefield where in 1380 Russians
won the first victory against the Mongolian invaders.

LEONTIEV, Constantine, 1831–1891: Author of several
novels. Original thinker and Russian diplomat in the Balkans.
Experienced a religious conversion in 1871 and came under the
influence of the Elder Amvrosy of Optino Monastery. He never
attained the inner peace he was looking for and was at odds
with other religious thinkers of his time.

MANSUROV, Sergei: Cultured Russian landowner who,
after the Revolution of 1917, became priest at quite a late age.
Was strongly opposed to Patriarch Sergius.

MECHEV, Father Alexei, 187?–1923: Rector of a Moscow
church (on "Maroseika" street) where a community was
formed under his guidance. He was assisted by his son, Father
Sergei Mechev, who was arrested and died in prison (1895–
1941).

MEREZHKOVSKY, Dimitri, 1865–1941: Russian author
of historical novels and essays in which he tried to reconcile
the spiritual heritage of paganism and Christianity. After the
Revolution of 1917 he emigrated to France.

NECTARY, Elder of Optino monastery, 1857–1928: Last
elder ("starets") of Optino Monastery from 1913 until the
closing down of the monastery. Died peacefully while living in
a private home.

NESTEROV, Mikhail, 1862–1942: Russian painter and illustrator. His works on the life of Saint Sergius of Radonezh can be seen at the Tretiakov Art Gallery in Moscow.

NOVOSELOV, M A, 1860–1938: Writer and publisher. Was a follower of Leo Tolstoy but later returned to the Orthodox Church. Was arrested in 1928 and condemned to 10 years of hard labor. In 1938 exiled to Siberia. No more news were received from him and the date of his death is unknown.

OPTINO MONASTERY: Well known Russian monastery where, through the influence of Father Paissi Velichkovsky (1725–1794) of Mount Athos and Moldavia, the practice of spiritual guidance by an "elder" was established. The best known "elder," or "staretz," of Optino monastery was Father Amvrosy.

PHILARET, Metropolitan of Moscow, 1782–1867: For almost fifty years was an active and firm administrator of the Russian Church.

PODVIG: The Russian word *podvig* means a heroic act. It is used by Church Fathers to describe spiritual or ascetic effort. A saint is called in Russian "podvizhnik," the one who carries on a *podvig*.

PROKEIMENON: A short verse from some psalm which is chanted during liturgical services before the reading of the Epistle or the Gospel.

ROSANOV, Vasili, 1856–1919: Writer of many religious works, though always with some negative reservations concerning Christianity. Friend of the leading Orthodox Christian thinkers of his time.

RUBLEV, Andrei, 1370?–1430: Celebrated Russian icon painter. Monk of the Holy Trinity monastery of St Sergius of Radonezh. His best known painting of the Holy Trinity is now exhibited at the Tretiakov Art Gallery in Moscow.

SAMIZDAT: Russian abbreviation meaning literally "selfpublishing." Term used to describe literary works that cannot be published in USSR and are privately typed or copied and passed around clandestinely.

SCHLICK, Father Michael: Disciple of Father Alexei Mechev. Ordained to priesthood in 1926. Arrested in 1927.

SERAPHIM, Father Seraphim Batugov: See *BATIUGOV*

SERGIUS (Stragorodsky), Metropolitan of Nizhni Novgorod and later Patriarch of All Russia: After Patriarch Tikhon's death the three bishops appointed by him as interim administrators were arrested and Metropolitan Sergius became deputy *locum tenens*. In 1927, in an attempt to legalize the position of the church, he proclaimed a "Declaration of loyalty to the Soviet government." This caused conflict and division within the Church. He became Patriarch in 1943 and died in 1944.

SILOUAN, Father Silouan of Mt Athos, 1866–1938: A Russian monk. Born in a peasant family he came to a monastery on Mount Athos and stayed there for 46 years.

SOBORNOST: Untranslatable Russian word derived from the word "sobor" or council. It is sometimes translated as "counciliarism," or "catholicity," or "spirit of fellowship."

SOLOUKHIN, Vladimir: Modern Soviet Russian author. In his book *Black Boards* he describes the adventures of a journalist looking for an ancient icon in the ruins of closed and destroyed churches.

SOLOVYEV, Vladimir, 1953–1900: Russian religious philosopher whose writings are full of mystical and eschatological overtones. Played an important part in the Russian religious philosophical revival of the early twentieth century.

STARETZ: Usually translated as "elder." A spiritually enlightened person, usually a monk and a priest, who assumes the spiritual guidance and counseling of his disciples.

STIKHERA: Church hymns chanted during Vespers and Matins in honor of a feast or a saint commemorated on that day.

SVENTITSKY, Father Valentin, 1881–1931: Was pastor of a Moscow church where in the nineteen twenties he attracted large crowds by his eloquent sermons. Was arrested in 1928 and sent to Siberia where he died in 1931.

THEOPHAN, Bishop Theophan the Recluse, 1815–1894: Took monastic vows at the age of 26, spent several years teaching in seminaries, was then ordained bishop. Retired in 1866 to the Vyshensky Monastery and became a recluse, devoting most of his time to correspondence with people who sought his guidance. Wrote several books on spiritual life which became classics. Was also interested in science and psychology.

TIKHON, Saint, of Zadonsk, 1724–1783: Born in a very poor clerical family and orphaned early, he experienced hardships in getting a seminary education. Was ordained bishop of Voronezh but soon retired to a monastery in Zadonsk. His writings and personal influence greatly influenced the spiritual life of Russia.

TROPARION: A short liturgical hymn describing the event celebrated on that day.

TYPIKON: Book containing rules and rubrics governing every aspect of church services.

VALAMO: Ancient Russian monastery on the islands of Lake Lagoda in Northern Russia, now transferred to Finland.

VASNETSOV, Victor, 1848–1926: Russian painter with a special interest in Russian early history. He painted murals for St Vladimir's Cathedral in Kiev, but had little understanding of ancient iconography. His brother, Apolinarius, specialized in painting ancient Russian street scenes.

VESTNIK: "Messenger" name of a magazine published by the Russian Christian Movement in Paris, France, since 1925. In recent years many writings of Orthodox Christian authors in the USSR have been published in the magazine and it seems to have considerable influence in the movement of religious revival there.

ZHIVOTSERKOVNIKI: Members of the so-called "Living Church" ("Zhivaya Tserkov"), a renovationist church group that in the twenties opposed Patriarch Tikhon and was supported by the Soviet Government.

ZVEZDINSKY, Bishop Seraphim, 1883–1937: Was born in

a priest's family and graduated from a seminary. Ordained bishop in 1919. Arrested in 1922 and exiled to the extreme north for two years. Opposed Patriarch Sergius. Was arrested again in 1926 and 1936 and executed in 1937.

ZYRYAN: Region in the extreme north-east part of Siberia.